THE AMBIGUOUS KINGDOM

INSIGHT INTO UNDERSTANDING THE GOSPEL OF THE KINGDOM AND ITS RELEVANCY FOR US TODAY

Published by Terry J. Boyle
Copyright © Terry John Boyle 2023.

Unless otherwise noted, all scripture quotations are taken from the Holy Bible, New King James Version Copyright © 1979, 1980, 1982
by Thomas Nelson, Inc.

All rights reserved. No part of this book may be reproduced in any form, stored in a retrieval system, or transmitted in any form by any means—electronic, mechanical, photocopy, recording or otherwise—without the prior written permission of the publisher, except as provided by Australian copyright law.

Words in capitals, or in bold or italics are the emphases
of the author Terry Boyle – terryjohnboyle@bigpond.com

Cover & typeset by Carl Butel at Deep Image – carl@deepimage.net.au

Cataloguing-in-Publication data is available from the
National Library of Australia.

ISBN 978-0-646-89253-5
eBook ISBN 978-0-646-89609-0

Acknowledgments

I thank my wife, Caroline, for her love, support, encouragement, and patience, especially while writing books. I also thank our children Amanda, Felicity, Andrew, Sharon, their spouses, and children for their support.

Our daughter Amanda, for her encouragement and input, and her husband Carl Butel, for the brilliant cover design and internal layout ready for printing.

I thank my son Andrew, a Baptist minister, for his excellent foreword, wise suggestions, valuable input, and encouragement.

I want to thank the leaders of various denominations for their fellowship and input into my life, especially during my many years of association with A2A.

To all the leaders and people of Papua New Guinea who have been a big part of our lives for many years. To the late John Pasterkamp, who led the work in PNG.

Thanks to the teaching and ministry of the late Hal Oxley and the late Trevor Chandler on the kingdom of God.

Thank you to all those at Centre Church in Lismore, NSW, where we ministered for twenty-one years before semi-retiring to the Gold Coast in Queensland, Australia, where we enjoy life at the time of writing.

CONTENTS

Foreword
Kingdom Quotes
Introduction

Ch 1. Why use the word ambiguous?

Ch 2. An unexpected kingdom

Ch 3. Laying a foundation for the kingdom

Ch 4. The King and His Kingdom

Ch 5. The parables of the kingdom

Ch 6. The kingdom code of conduct

Ch 7. The early church and the kingdom

Ch 8. Paul explains and expands the kingdom

Ch 9. The substance of the kingdom

Ch 10. Is the kingdom relevant for us today?

Ch 11. The kingdom and modernity

Ch 12. The kingdom is a word in season

Ch 13. Your kingdom come your will be done

Ch 14. Missions and the gospel of the kingdom

Ch 15. When can we expect the coming kingdom?

Ch 16. How will the King and His Kingdom return?

Ch 17. As you see the day approaching

THE AMBIGUOUS KINGDOM

Foreword

When Dad asked me to consider writing a foreword for this book, my initial reaction was to decline, suggesting that there must be others more qualified and with more to offer on this subject. However, on further reflection, I realised that being a son makes me uniquely qualified. I have seen firsthand that the concepts in Dad's books are not just borrowed theories or aspirational ideologies but spiritual realities that can bear fruit through obedience to Jesus.

Growing up, some of my fondest memories of my father were of him preaching inspired sermons and praying over people with conviction and authority in the Holy Spirit. I think those early impressions left an indelible mark on my young heart, encouraging me, together with my upbringing in a lovely Christian home, to surrender to Jesus myself and pursue my pathway into vocational ministry.

When I read the manuscript of this book, I was impressed by three things: the approach taken, the subjects covered, and the appeal to primary sources, namely Jesus' direct teaching on the kingdom.

In taking the title 'The Ambiguous Kingdom,' Dad sums up what for many believe is somewhat of an enigma, in that the kingdom of God was the main thing Jesus emphasised in His earthly teaching, yet is one of the least understood aspects of Christian theology.

What is the kingdom exactly? Where is it? Is it literal? Is it purely spiritual? Has it come? Is it coming? What is the difference between the kingdom and the church? Where is our place in it? The search for answers to this question of ambiguity forms the primary approach to writing this book. In addressing these difficult questions, many subjects are covered, and they are done more or less chronologically, from the foundations of the kingdom right through to the final manifestation of the kingdom. I found this helpful in building a layer-by-layer understanding of the kingdom. One of the main strengths of this book for me was the regular inclusion of many direct teachings of Jesus on the kingdom.

This book is a testimony to my father's life and ministry as he grew deeper in his understanding of the kingdom. May it serve as a timely reminder of the significance of the kingdom of God and its relevance to us today.

Rev. Andrew Boyle, M.Div.

Associate Pastor of Fairfield Christian Family Church, Brisbane, Australia

Kingdom Quotes

"Sometimes I am so focused on the "not yet" of the kingdom of God that I miss the "now" of it – too."

– Sarah Bessey

"The seeking of the kingdom of God is the chief business of the Christian life."

– Jonathan Edwards

"Men and women of caution never advanced the frontiers of the kingdom of God."

– J. Oswald Sanders

"For He has rescued us from the kingdom of darkness and transferred us into the kingdom of His dear Son who purchased our freedom and forgave our sins."

– The Apostle Paul

THE AMBIGUOUS KINGDOM

Introduction

For many years, I found the subject of the "Kingdom of God" ambiguous and a challenge to understand its relevance for us today.

Whenever I heard preachers discuss the kingdom of God, it seemed to be a vague, nebulous theme that needed clarification.

I felt led to study the subject diligently because Jesus continually preached on the kingdom of God. I did this by doing a thesis for my Bachelor of Ministry on "Missions and the Gospel of the Kingdom."

As you can imagine, I read many books and commentaries besides studying the scriptures. I was amazed at what I discovered about why the scriptures appeared ambiguous and nebulous. I also became very excited to learn how important and relevant this subject is for us today.

My son, Andrew, has a copy of my thesis and said in passing, "Dad, you could turn this into another book." I already hold Andrew responsible for encouraging me to write my last book, "But for the Grace of God Go I." So here we go again; I hope you enjoy it and gain a better understanding of the gospel of the kingdom.

Chapter 1

Why use the word ambiguous?

Why did I choose the word *ambiguous* in the title of this book? As I mentioned in my introduction, for many years as a Christian, I found the subject of the "Kingdom of God" ambiguous. It seemed to lack substance, and I could not get my head around its actual relevance.

According to Wikipedia's definition, "The word ambiguity is the type of meaning by which a phrase, statement, or resolution is not clearly defined, making for several interpretations; others describe it as a concept or statement that has no real reference. A common aspect of ambiguity is uncertainty."

I also felt it was vague and nebulous and lacked clarification and practical application for us today. Because of the spiritual nature of the kingdom of God, it appeared to be invisible, and there was nothing tangible I could hang my hat on.

I considered using the title "The Visible King and the

Invisible Kingdom." However, the King who was visible on earth is now invisible most of the time, and the invisible kingdom is now visible in its spiritual form through the church. If you are a little confused, you are not alone.

I know others who have wrestled with this dilemma, not only those relatively new to the Christian faith but also some who have been Christians for many years, still struggle to understand the complexities of the kingdom of God.

Robert Farrar Capon, in his book, "Kingdom, Grace, Judgment," says, "The mystery of the kingdom, it seems, is a radical mystery: even when you tell people about it in so many words, it remains permanently intractable to all their attempts to make sense of it."

We often find something ambiguous because we do not have the context of the whole story. We could say, "The punch made him dizzy." That would be ambiguous because we do not know why the punch made him dizzy. Did someone punch him, or was it the punch he drank? Another example is "I saw her duck." Did I see her dodge a punch, or did I see her pet duck? We can misinterpret the outcome if we do not have the full context. It is a bit like this when we try to figure out the kingdom of God.

In his book "Managing Transitions," William Bridges discusses the capacity to live within the discomfort of ambiguity. "If we can live with ambiguity, change and transition can be constructive and life-giving. If not, it can be threatening, disruptive, and even destructive."

On the positive side

However, there is a positive side to ambiguity regarding the kingdom of God. It can be valuable because godliness is a mystery, and we must open it up for more investigation and discussion. Life would be boring if everything were so cut and dry, and we would have nothing to explore and discuss. So, ambiguity leaves plenty of room for stimulating interpretation.

Ambiguity can be considered a literary tool. A good author is not content with telling you the plot or the outcome upfront without allowing you to work it out by drawing inferences and conclusions.

The more intriguing the plot appears, the more we are inclined to glean information from others' thoughts and views to help us construct a satisfactory summary.

The ambiguity surrounding the kingdom of God is a complex interplay of linguistic, religious and cultural factors. It invites exploration, interpretation and observation rather than a clear-cut conclusion.

After I studied the subject in depth and wrote a thesis on "Missions and the Gospel of the Kingdom," I began to understand its complexities.

I may not have all the answers, but I have some understanding, which should help you and give some insight into the reality of the kingdom of God.

The search for a better world

Throughout the centuries, man has searched for a better world—dreaming of a utopia in the face of persecution, oppression, and depravity. The Bible promises a Messiah to set up that better world - the Kingdom of God.

> *"For unto us a Child is born, unto us a Son is given; and the government will be upon His shoulder…Of the increase of His government and peace, there shall be no end."*
>
> Isaiah 9:6-7.

Jesus will fulfil the second part of this verse when He comes again. So, when Jesus preached that the time was fulfilled, it was only the beginning of the fulfilment of the promised kingdom of God.

> *"The time is fulfilled, and the kingdom of God is at hand. Repent, and believe in the gospel."*
>
> Mark 1:15.

Jesus declared that the anticipated promise of a Messiah for Israel had finally arrived. He proclaimed the kingdom of God to be the answer for humanity. This is why the proclamation of the kingdom of God is so important. It now gives people a better and eternal alternative to this world system.

Spreading the message

> *Jesus said, "This gospel of the kingdom will be preached in all the world as a witness to all the nations, and then the end will come."*
>
> Matthew 24:14.

Why use the word ambiguous?

Do we grasp the gravity of this declaration? It is a message that will continue to be proclaimed by preachers, Christians, churches, mission organisations, and missionaries of all nations to all nations until the end of time as we know it. Jesus makes it a priority.

Today, we know it is possible to reach the world with the gospel because of the printed page, the computer, and modern technology. We have the capacity and resources to reach every kindred tongue, tribe, and nation.

As a missionary in Papua New Guinea, I witnessed the gospel reaching tribes in remote areas despite dense jungles, rugged mountains, and isolated islands. It all began with pioneer missionaries who were sometimes willing to lay down their lives for the gospel's sake.

I remember going to several remote areas where we walked for miles, trudged through jungles, waded through rivers, and climbed mountains until we came to a primitive village to preach the gospel.

On one occasion, we went to a remote area in the majestic rugged Highlands of PNG. I had been pre-warned by the nationals that they had a custom in this village when they greeted you to quickly put their hand between your legs to check out your genitals.

Even though I had been pre-warned, it certainly took me by surprise. The gospel had not only reached these people, but they had also built a makeshift church made out of bush materials.

In the last two paragraphs, you may have noticed that I have only used the word gospel, not the gospel of the kingdom. I think we are inclined to do this. Jesus could have just used the word gospel, but He mainly spoke of the gospel of the kingdom.

Why did He emphasise the word kingdom?

The kingdom of God can refer to different phases, such as how it was before Christ (the Kingdom of Israel in the Old Testament), the kingdom introduced by Christ here and now, and the kingdom still to come at Christ's return, which we are all currently waiting for.

Do we understand it all?

Understanding the complexities of the kingdom of God is often challenging. Why does Matthew use the phrase kingdom of heaven instead of the kingdom of God, as in Mark, Luke, and the epistles? It is thought that Matthew's gospel was directed at the Jews, and he was trying to avoid using the word God, which was considered to be holy and not to be used lightly, which may have offended some Jews. However, most scholars feel the two phrases are theologically identical. Speaking to the rich young ruler, Matthew records Jesus using the kingdom of heaven and the kingdom of God interchangeably. *(Matthew 19:23-24)*.

But I will take a moment to throw the cat among the pigeons by raising other scriptures that are just as challenging to understand as those related to God's kingdom. For example, the phrase, *"We sit together in heavenly places in Christ*

Why use the word ambiguous?

Jesus." This cannot be taken literally as in the flesh but refers to our spiritual state.

> *"Even when we were dead in trespasses, made us alive together with Christ (by grace you have been saved) and raised us up together, and made us sit together in the heavenly places in Christ Jesus?"*
>
> Ephesians 2:5-6.

It speaks of our spiritual position of authority in Christ and His kingdom. All things are under His feet (and our feet) in Christ, which means we have authority over the powers of darkness.

Maybe we are not meant to fully understand some of these things as long as we accept them by faith and use these spiritual truths to overcome the opposition we face.

We just read, *"By grace, you have been saved."* So, why not just preach a message of salvation through grace and faith in Christ? Is it necessary to focus on the kingdom of God? Will it make any difference? What is so significant about the message of the gospel of the kingdom?

I want us to understand the kingdom of God better as we explore the scriptures relating to Jesus, the apostles, and the early church in apostolic times and their interpretations of the kingdom.

I will also try to clarify what seems to be an ambiguous kingdom and its relevance for us today. We will discover why the powerful message of the gospel of the kingdom should become a priority for the church.

May it become a more desired theme to proclaim and relevant enough for people to want to be born again into the kingdom of God through faith in Christ.

Chapter 2

An unexpected kingdom

We become very disappointed when we anticipate something that turns out differently from what we have been expecting.

Some years ago, I ordered a new silver-coloured Ford Falcon sedan. After waiting several months for it, I went to pick it up from the showroom, and they unveiled a dark grey one. When I protested that I had ordered a silver one, the salesman was apologetic and gave me some flimsy excuse that he was colour-blind and had made a mistake. Rather than wait another three months, I accepted it but never overcame my disappointment.

We must understand that the kingdom Jesus introduced was not what the Jewish leaders expected. They would have been disappointed, hoping for a political or military-style kingdom, which would have been more in keeping with their understanding of the coming Messiah.

Jesus' proclamation of the kingdom differed because He

emphasised its present reality. Jesus spoke of a kingdom in spiritual terms, being within people, emphasising humility and service, associating with sinners and outcasts, and having a universal appeal.

Jesus spoke of servanthood and humility to defuse an issue among the disciples' quest for greatness.

> *"You know the rulers of the Gentiles rule it over them, and those who are great exercise authority over them. Yet it shall not be so among you; but whoever desires to become great among you, let him be your servant. And whoever desires to be first among you, let him be your slave - just as the Son of Man did not come to be served, but to serve, and to give His life a ransom for many."*
>
> Matthew 20:25-28.

This would have challenged the thinking and expectations of the religious people at that time.

The seed of David

God had made a promise to David.

> *"When your days are fulfilled, and you rest with your fathers, I will set up your seed after you, who will come from your body, and I will establish his kingdom. He shall build a house for My name, and I will establish the throne of his kingdom forever."*
>
> 2 Samuel 7:12-13.

So, the rabbinic expectation of a long-awaited- Messiah was that He would come and re-establish the Davidic kingdom.

He would establish himself as king and rule from his throne in Jerusalem, the capital of Israel. He was to be a direct descendant of King David.

The message from the angel Gabriel to Mary seems, in part, to confirm this expectation.

> *"Then the angel said to her, "Do not be afraid, Mary, for you have found favour with God. And behold, you will conceive in your womb and bring forth a Son, and you shall call His name Jesus. He will be great and will be called the son of the Highest, and the Lord God will give Him the throne of His Father David. And He will reign over the house of Jacob forever, and of His kingdom, there will be no end."*
>
> Luke 1:30-33.

It was only feasible that there was an expectation that these prophetic words were about to be fulfilled.

Jesus was the Messiah

If we consider the genealogy of Jesus as in Matthew chapter one, we have the right person in the right place at the right time. Jesus was the Messiah. But He did not fit the image they were expecting.

> *"Rejoice greatly, O daughter of Zion! Shout, O, daughter of Jerusalem! Behold, your king is coming to you; He is just and having salvation, lowly and riding on a donkey, a colt, the foal of a donkey."*
>
> Zechariah 9:9.

Although Jesus fulfilled this prophecy, He was not the kind of king they sought. Perhaps they expected someone riding in a chariot with flames of fire pulled by a white horse.

I remember some years ago, a would-be preacher came and told me he saw himself preaching on the platform of our church, dressed in a white suit and white shoes. I did not understand what he was trying to say, except that he wanted to perform and be the centre of attention. I did not share his enthusiasm, so it did not happen.

Jesus did not fit the image of the Messiah everyone anticipated. He wore no crown, had no palace, and no army. All He had was a mixed band of disciples, some of whom would have been branded radical troublemakers.

A disappointed John the Baptist

John the Baptist, who referred to Jesus as "The Lamb of God who takes away the sin of the world" (John 1:29), had expected Jesus to establish His kingdom. When there seemed to be no evidence of this happening, John sent two disciples to Jesus to ask if He was the one or if they should look for another.

> *"When John heard in prison about the works of Christ, he sent two of his disciples and said to Him, "Are you the one or do we look for another?"*
>
> Matthew 11:2-3.

John must have wondered about Jesus because he was

expecting the Messiah to deliver them from Roman Rule and establish the kingdom of God.

When the disciples of John asked Jesus, "Are you the one, or do we look for another?" Jesus answered and said to them.

"Go and tell John the things which you hear and see; "The blind see and the lame walk; the lepers are cleansed and the deaf hear; the dead are raised up, and the poor have the gospel preached to them." "And blessed is he who is not offended because of Me."

Matthew 11:4-6.

Jesus must have sensed that John was offended and disappointed. "Go and tell him what you see and hear." Jesus probably thought John knew the prophetic scriptures about the Messiah well enough to realise that only the Messiah could perform such miracles, which would hopefully satisfy John.

However, John probably thought there would be some indication that Jesus was setting up His kingdom. Maybe he expected Jesus to become king and set him free from prison. However, Jesus showed no aggression toward the Roman Empire; instead, he was aggressive toward the religious leaders because of their hypocrisy.

The religious leaders

The religious leaders of the day expected Jesus to be more aggressive toward the Romans than toward them as the Messiah.

Jesus' message was one of repentance. He directed his aggression toward the devil and a corrupt Jewish religious system, like when He drove the money changers out of the temple.

> *"Then Jesus went into the temple of God and drove out all those who bought and sold in the temple and overturned the tables of the money changers and the seats of those who sold doves. And He said to them, "It is written, "My house shall be called a house of prayer, but you have made it a den of thieves." Then the blind and the lame came to Him in the temple, and He healed them."*
>
> Matthew 21:12-14.

The religious leaders reacted. They were jealous of His popularity and following and turned against Jesus and His followers.

In Matthew 23, we have a whole chapter where Jesus verbally attacks the scribes and the Pharisees, calling them hypocrites. They were putting on a show outwardly expecting people to uphold the law but were guilty themselves of failing to do so.

A kingdom not of this world

Jesus had no intention of taking up arms against anyone. We see this when they came to arrest Him, and Peter drew his sword and struck the servant of the high priest and cut off his ear. Jesus told him to put his sword away, and He healed the servant's ear.

In response, Jesus rebuked Peter and said,

"Do you think that I cannot now pray to my Father, and He will provide Me with more than twelve legions of angels? How, then, could the scriptures be fulfilled that it must happen thus?"

Matthew 26:53-54.

Jesus had a different agenda and knew the cross came before the throne. But this was not what the people were expecting.

In response to Pilate asking Jesus if He was king of the Jews, Jesus answered,

"My kingdom is not of this world. If my kingdom were of this world, my servants would fight so that I should not be delivered to the Jews, but now My kingdom is not from here."

John 18:36.

Jesus is saying if His kingdom were of this world, my servants would fight. There would be civil unrest and war against the Romans. But that was not what His kingdom was going to do. Jesus had to go to the cross to fulfil all the prophetic scriptures.

Crucified as king of the Jews

If this Jesus was the Messiah, the Jews were bitterly disappointed. The crucifixion was not part of what they had expected to see. They thought they would see an insurrection, not a crucifixion.

In Matthew 27:37, we read the sign above His head on the cross was written the inscription -

"THIS IS JESUS KING OF THE JEWS"

When Jesus hung on the cross, he was on display publicly and put to shame. It looked like the one who called himself the Messiah was a defeated king, and as a result, many, including the Jewish religious leaders, mocked Him.

> *"And those who passed by blasphemed Him, wagging their heads and saying, "You who destroy the temple and build it in three days save Yourself. If you are the Son of God, come down from the cross." Likewise, the chief priests, also mocking with the scribes and elders, said, "He saved others; Himself He cannot save. If He is king of Israel. Let Him come down from the cross now, and we will believe Him."*

Matthew 27:39-42.

Why did He stay on the cross?

When Jesus hung on the cross, those who passed by cried, "If He is king of Israel, let Him come down from the cross."

He could have called upon angels and miraculously stepped down from the cross. But Jesus could not do that, and there would be no calling upon twelve legions of angels to deliver Him. He had to die and shed His blood as the Lamb of God to atone for the sins of the human race; otherwise, there would be no salvation or eternal life.

The cross was something the Jews could not comprehend. They did not understand that there needed to be a cross before a crown. So, unfortunately, many Jews to this day still mock Jesus and Christianity. They did not understand that the resurrection, the ascension, and the eventual return of Christ would come after the cross.

Jesus died for every person

Jesus died for every single person. When He cried, "It is finished on the cross," He meant it. Sin has been dealt with once and for all.

> *"For the love of Christ compels us, because we judge thus: that if One died for all, then all died; and he died for all, that those who live should no longer live for themselves, but for Him who died for them and rose again."*
>
> 2 Corinthians 5:14-15.

It does not matter who you are or what you have done. Your sin has been dealt with at the cross. You must accept that by faith and live for Christ, for He has tasted death for every man. (Hebrews 2:9).

Jesus' resurrection and ascension

The book of Acts begins with the fact that Jesus rose from the dead and is very much alive.

> *"He also presented Himself alive after His suffering by many infallible proofs, being seen by them during forty days and speaking of things pertaining to the kingdom of God"*
>
> Acts 1:3.

While the disciples were watching, Jesus was taken up in a cloud out of sight, ascending back to heaven, and two angels appeared to them, saying -

"Men of Galilee, why do you stand gazing up into heaven? This same Jesus who was taken up from you into heaven will so come in like manner as you saw Him go to heaven."

Acts 1:11.

So, what the Jews were looking for as the Messiah to come and establish His kingdom did come, but not as they expected. But He is still yet to come. We will continue to elaborate on these thoughts.

Chapter 3

Laying a foundation for the kingdom

Whenever someone builds a structure, they must first lay a proper foundation. A lot of time goes into getting the foundation right.

Some years ago, my wife Caroline wanted me to build a pergola as an extension to our back veranda for her plant display. Knowing my limitations, I was very reluctant, but she insisted that I at least try it.

I needed to start with a firm foundation, so I measured it according to a rough plan and made a makeshift structure according to my measurements.

I was not even close; it would have looked ridiculous. As a science and maths teacher, my wife came to the rescue. She calculated the right height and placement for the stirrups for the uprights that I was about to place in the concrete to give it a sure foundation.

To this day, I do not understand how she worked it out with such precision. But when we finished, it looked great and was a lovely addition and feature to our house. It looked so good that it became a talking point, and I would claim it as my masterpiece, which would provoke my wife to have her say and let people know who got the foundation right. But with any project in life, getting the foundation correct is so important.

Despite living in an unpredictable, insecure, and unstable world, the kingdom of God is on a firm foundation that world events cannot shake.

"Therefore, since we have received a kingdom that cannot be shaken, let us have grace, by which we may serve God acceptably with reverence and godly fear. For our God is a consuming fire."

Hebrews 12:28-29.

The kingdom of God is unshakable. The foundation for it apart from Christ may vary depending on religious and theological perspectives, leading to diverse interpretations. Some examples may include justice and righteousness, love and compassion, mercy and grace. But I would like to highlight justice and righteousness.

John the Baptist began to lay the foundation for the kingdom of God by preaching a message of repentance in preparation for the coming Messiah.

> *"In those days, John the Baptist came preaching in the wilderness of Judea, and saying, "Repent for the kingdom of heaven is at hand!" For this is he who was spoken by the prophet Isaiah, saying: "The voice of one crying in the wilderness: Prepare the way of the Lord; Make His paths straight."*

> Matthew 3:1-3.

Justice and righteousness

Justice is the quality of being fair and impartial and treating people equitably, particularly the marginalised, oppressed, and vulnerable. It is closely related to righteousness, which is more about moral uprightness and living according to the word of God.

John the Baptist confronted and challenged all those who were self righteous. When he saw many of the Pharisees and Sadducees coming to his baptism, he said to them -

> *"Brood of vipers! Who warned you to flee from the wrath to come? Therefore, bear fruits worthy of repentance."*

> Matthew 3:7-8.

When Jesus came to John to be baptised by him, John hesitated and said, "I need to be baptised by you." But Jesus answered and said to Him,

> *"Permit it to be so now, for thus it is fitting for us to fulfil all righteousness."*

> Matthew 3:14-15.

His righteousness

When Jesus told His disciples to *"Seek first the kingdom of God and His righteousness, and all these things shall be added unto you."* – Matthew 6:33. He was giving them a key to understanding kingdom righteousness which is in Him. His righteousness not self righteousness like the Scribes and Pharisees or righteousness based on trying to keep the law of Moses.

It is this kind of righteousness that is also the sceptre the king will use to rule over His kingdom.

> *"But to the Son, He says, "Your throne, O God, is forever and ever; A sceptre of righteousness is the sceptre of Your kingdom."*
>
> Hebrews 1:8.

Such a sceptre is an emblem of authority, power, and rulership. God will rule from His throne with a sceptre of righteousness. But how can we justify righteousness without becoming like the religious leaders Jesus faced? We do not want to become like the self-righteous religious system of the scribes and Pharisees.

Jesus warned His disciples by saying -

> *"For I say to you, that unless your righteousness exceeds the righteousness of the scribes and Pharisees, you will by no means enter the kingdom of heaven."*
>
> Matthew 5:20.

What a shock it must have been for the religious leaders

when Jesus confronted them this way. But how can we have righteousness without legalism?

Paul explains righteousness

Paul compares God's righteousness to the zealous, legalistic, self-righteous Israelites. There is a vast difference between the two.

"For they are being ignorant of God's righteousness, and seeking to establish their own righteousness, have not submitted to the righteousness of God. For Christ is the end of the law for righteousness to everyone who believes."

Romans 10:1-4.

In the context of God, righteousness is that innate part of Him that is always morally right, pure, and perfectly just. Our righteousness is our attempt to be like this, but we fall spectacularly short. The Pharisees were self-righteous, believing they were righteous, often through works, but they deceived themselves.

Our attempts at righteousness (apart from God) can only be considered as self-righteous works. Even our 'very best' attempts are corrupted and unacceptable to God.

That is why we need a righteousness apart from ourselves, the righteousness of God. As Christians, we are made the righteousness of God in Christ. We can never make ourselves righteous.

"Therefore, if anyone is in Christ, he is a new creation; old things

> have passed away; behold all things have become new.... For He made Him who knew no sin to be sin for us, that we might become the righteousness of God in Him."

2 Corinthians 5:17 and 21.

As new creations, we have become God's righteousness in Christ. However, we may not feel that we are righteous as we still wrestle with the flesh, which tries to dominate our lives and make us feel unworthy of His righteousness. Our old legalistic, self-righteous ways do not belong in the kingdom.

How to build on this foundation

Paul warns us to be careful how we build upon the foundation of Christ and the kingdom of God, which Jesus has laid for us.

> *"According to the grace of God which is given to me, as a wise master builder, I have laid the foundation, and another, builds on it, but let each one take heed how he builds on it. For no other foundation can anyone lay that which is laid, which is Jesus Christ.*
>
> *Now, if anyone builds on the foundation with gold, silver, precious stones, wood, hay, or straw, each one's work will become clear, for the day will declare it because it will be revealed by fire, and the fire will test each one's work of what sort it is. If anyone's work, which he has built on endures, he will receive a reward. If anyone's work is burned, he will suffer loss; but he himself will be saved, yet so as through fire."*

1 Corinthians 3:10-14.

I suggest that things that burn, like wood, hay, and straw,

represent carnal self-righteous works. Earlier in this chapter, he refers to carnal things like pride, envy, strife, and division. These things do not belong in the church or the kingdom of God. You might think you are in trouble if you battle with some of these things. You may lose your reward but not your salvation.

Gospel and kingdom

If we are to believe in this unshakable kingdom, we need to understand the link between the gospel and the kingdom.

We will examine the New Testament Greek and Old Testament Hebrew to gain a foundational understanding of the words gospel and kingdom as Jesus declared them.

When Jesus preaches the gospel of the kingdom in Matthew 24:23, The word gospel can be translated from the Greek *euangelion* as good news derived from *euanggelizos*, which means to evangelise. An ancient usage of euangelion makes it reasonably pointed towards the kingdom. When a new ruler or king conquered a people, a herald would proclaim the Evangelion (in every township) that a new king ruled over the land. For Jesus and the apostles to use euangelion tapped into this usage, and for the people listening, the gospel was the proclamation of a new king, and the heralds were Jesus and his followers – now us as Christians.

The Greek word for kingdom is *basileia*, which implies royalty, a place of power, a sovereign, and a king who rules a realm or region.

The Hebrew word for kingdom is almost identical; it is from the Hebrew root *malkuth*, which means to rule over a realm from a throne.

So, when Jesus preached the gospel of the kingdom, He was preaching the good news and demonstrating it by ruling over sin, sickness, and demonic powers. It was evangelism at its best as multitudes began to follow Him.

George Eldon Ladd, in his book, "The Gospel of the Kingdom," sums it up this way –

"The primary meaning of the Hebrew word *malkuth* in the Old Testament and of the Greek word basilica in the New Testament is the rank authority and sovereignty exercised by a king. A basilica is a realm over which a sovereign exercises authority. It may be the people who belong to that realm and over whom authority is exercised, but these are secondary-derived meanings. A kingdom is the authority to rule, the king's sovereignty. The kingdom of God is His Kingship, His Rule, His Authority."

Graeme Holdsworth, in his book "Gospel and Kingdom," puts it similarly -

"We best understand this concept in terms of the relationship of a Ruler to subjects. There is a king who rules, a people who are ruled, and a sphere where this rule is recognised as taking place.

Put another way, the kingdom of God involves –

(a) God's people.

(b) In God's place.

(c) Under God's rule."

However, it all begins within the heart. It is all about His kingship and our obedience to His rule in our hearts. Albert Schweitzer said, "There can be no kingdom of God in the world without the kingdom of God in our hearts."

When Jesus preached the gospel, he was preaching the good news, the best news that anybody could hope to hear.

The long-awaited kingdom of God is here now. It is a kingdom far superior to any other on earth, where almighty God will eventually reign for eternity.

"The Lord has established His throne in heaven, and His kingdom rules over all."

Psalm 103:19.

It is forever expanding

This gospel of the kingdom is forever expanding. People respond to the gospel by putting their faith in Christ for salvation. It is a continual ongoing process.

As the senior pastor in Lismore, NSW, Australia, I remember becoming frustrated when the church was not growing as I thought it should.

We would gain people, and then they would move on

because it was a rural area. They would gravitate to capital cities for education and work.

As I prayed, the Lord reassured me not to worry about the church's growth because His kingdom was still growing and expanding as people came through our church and then moved on to other areas. They often gravitated to other churches experiencing growth or new churches being planted.

In Luke 13:18-19, Jesus explains how the kingdom of God expands through a parable. We will devote a whole chapter to kingdom parables, but I need to point out how the kingdom of God begins so tiny and ends up so huge.

"What is the kingdom like, and to what shall I compare it? It is like a mustard seed, which a man took and put in his garden, and it grew and became a large tree."

The kingdom of God is described as an insignificant, tiny seed that is hardly visible, yet it eventually becomes a massive tree.

In fact, it ends up covering the whole earth. In the book of Daniel (2:31-45), King Nebuchadnezzar of Babylon dreams of a great statue made of various materials, such as gold, silver, iron, bronze, and clay. In a dream, a stone, 'cut without hands', strikes the statue on its feet, causing it to crumble, and then the stone grows into a great mountain, filling the whole earth.

Daniel interprets the vision. The different materials represent different kingdoms and empires throughout history.

The stone that is 'cut without hands' and strikes the statue, causing it to crumble, represents the kingdom of God. When the kingdom of God fully comes, all other kingdoms will be destroyed, and the kingdom of God will rule over all.

So, whatever we may see through church growth, the kingdom of God is forever expanding worldwide and will continue to do so until Christ returns.

What the kingdom is not and is

It is not of this world. Jesus said to Pilate -

> *"My kingdom is not of this world…" Pilate, therefore, said to Him, "Are you a king then?" Jesus said, "You say rightly that I am a king. For this cause, I was born, and for this cause, I have come into the world."*
>
> John 18:36-37.

Jesus said, *"For this cause, I was born, and for this cause, I have come into the world."* What cause is He referring to? He came to be King.

But first, He had to come as the Lamb of God to die on the cross for our sins. The Jews were disappointed because they expected the Messiah would come and establish a literal kingdom and deliver them from Roman rule.

However, there will come a day when Jesus will return to this earth as the King of Kings and the Lord of Lords (Revelation 19:16). But the time is not yet.

THE AMBIGUOUS KINGDOM

Many people find the kingdom of God ambiguous because it is not materialistic. It is spiritual and appears to be somewhat invisible.

Chapter 4

The King and His Kingdom

Jesus, as the king of His kingdom, is central to Christian theology. His kingship is expressed in His teachings, miracles and, ultimately, through His death, resurrection, and ascension.

Christians believe that one day, Jesus will return in glory to establish His kingdom fully on earth. This is referred to as the second coming of Christ.

A king must have a kingdom and a single sovereign ruler. A kingdom can also be known as a monarchy, in which one person, a king or queen, usually rules the kingdom over their subjects by birth.

From a Christian perspective, talking about the kingdom of God ultimately means that Jesus is king, the sovereign Lord of the universe, and the supreme ruler overall.

The Jews became convicted when Peter preached on

the day of Pentecost. Some realised they had crucified the Messiah, the Christ, or anointed one ordained to be their king and ruler of the universe.

> *"Therefore, let all the house of Israel know assuredly that God has made this Jesus, whom you crucified both Lord and Christ."*
>
> Acts 2:36.

In doing so, they had separated Christ from His kingdom, meaning there would ultimately be no king or kingdom. They realised they had made a colossal mistake if He was the Messiah. So, many repented and became Christians.

Most kingdoms on earth adopt the king's vision and, to some extent, characteristics. The kingdom of God is no different.

Philip said to Him, *"Lord, show us the Father, and it is sufficient for us." Jesus said to him… "He who has seen Me has seen the Father. "…. "Do you not believe that I am in the Father, and the Father is in Me?"* John 14:8-9.

We could also say the same about Jesus and His kingdom. If you have seen Jesus, you have seen His kingdom, for they are inseparable.

E. Stanley Jones came to this conclusion, which led him to change the title of a book he was writing.

He claims – "When I saw the person of Christ was just as important as the message of Christ – the Kingdom of God. The two were linked, inseparably linked. So, in midstream,

I had to change horses. Instead of emphasising the order, I had to make both of them my message – the order and the person. So, I had to change the title of the book from "The Laws, Principles, and Attitudes of the Kingdom of God" to "The Unshakable Kingdom and the Unchanging Person" (a book I highly recommend). I would suggest the kingdom of God has come in the person, the word, and the works of Jesus.

While on the mission field in Papua New Guinea, we led an Australian Navy Officer to the Lord. He invited us to join his family at a Navy lineup in Port Moresby to meet Prince Charles (now King Charles) at the Australian Navy Base in Port Moresby.

We were delighted, and we waited in anticipation with much excitement. There was a lot of nervous tension as we waited, and waited, and waited.

However, because Prince Charles was running so late, his motorcade drove straight past the base, much to our disappointment.

That is the closest I have come to meeting royalty, except the night I was born again and met Jesus. He dwells with me, is in me through the Holy Spirit, and is my eternal Lord and King.

Since Charles became king of the British Empire, I have noticed that you are inclined to hear more about him than you do about his kingdom. The point is they are inseparable. He may not run the everyday affairs of the kingdom, but he is the only sovereign at the moment entitled to sit upon the British throne. His son, William, Prince of Wales, will eventually succeed Charles.

As a matter of interest, Queen Victoria became the ruler of the British Empire and ruled from 1837 to 1901. Not long after her death, a story in a London newspaper highlighted her faith in Christ. After a sermon, she approached the speaker and said, "Oh, how I wished that the Lord might come during my lifetime." When he asked her what her desire was based on, she replied, "I should like to lay my crown at His feet."

However, all the kingdoms of this earth are subject to becoming unstable and changeable. But not the Kingdom of God; it is unshakable, absolute, and ruled by the unchanging person of Christ.

Kingdom values without a king

Today's world wants the kingdom of God's values without the King. In an informative podcast, a cultural analyst, Mark Sayers, argues that culture has three stages -

"There is the pre-Christian culture in which superstition and paganism dominated how people view life and the afterlife."

"Then Christianity came (the second culture) and secularised the world of myth and legend. Christianity is creedal in nature, affirming a unique view of God, mankind and creation."

"Now, we live in a culture that is increasingly defining itself as post-Christian. This third culture is still built on many of the philosophical assumptions the second culture established but defines itself in opposition to and against Christianity. Today, Western culture may be thought of as wanting all the kingdom's benefits without accepting the king's authority. That is, today we want many of the values that Jesus spoke of and taught but we refuse to acknowledge the authority of the one who gives them. We want the kingdom without THE KING."

This is so true, but from a Christian perspective, we cannot have one without the other.

Jesus introduces His Kingdom

Jesus introduces His kingdom in Matthew 4:17, saying, *"Repent for the kingdom of heaven is at hand."* His immediate challenge to all is to "repent."

The word repent comes from the Greek metanoia, which means thinking differently or changing your mind and direction. I completely changed my mind and direction when I committed my life to Christ. Before becoming a Christian, as a young teenager, my passion was to play 'Aussie Rules' football and establish a successful business to enjoy a comfortable lifestyle. I thought I had it all mapped out. But God had something else in mind.

After a severe knee injury, I had an encounter with Christ, and through unusual circumstances, I came to faith in Christ. I responded to God's call on my life to serve Christ in ministry, a decision I have not once regretted. But you do not have to give up your career to become a dedicated follower of Christ.

When Jesus preached repentance, He gave people the opportunity to find another alternative to the cruel and brutal Roman Empire. Although repentance involves a sort of death, we gain so much more by following Christ.

Jesus gives everyone a chance to enter the Kingdom of God. However, they must repent.

Kingdom power on display

Jesus does not waste any time demonstrating the power of the gospel of the kingdom.

In Matthew 4:23, we read, *"Jesus went about all Galilee teaching in their synagogues preaching the gospel of the kingdom and healing all kinds of sickness and all kinds of disease among the people. Then His fame went throughout all Syria; and they brought to Him all sick people who were afflicted with various diseases and torments and those who were demon-possessed, epileptics, and paralytics, and He healed them."*

He ruled over demons that tormented people. He ministered in a supernatural realm, but this was only the beginning of his ministry.

He continued demonstrating His power to rule over spiritual forces, sickness, disease, storms, and natural events; He even raised the dead.

Being born again

The King and His Kingdom

I once had an angry neighbour tell me he was accosted down the street by those "born agains" who tried to convert him. He knew they were Christians and what they were trying to do, but he had no understanding of what it meant to be born again.

Jesus explains what it means to be born again through His dialogue with Nicodemus, a devout religious leader. He was a Pharisee and a ruler of the Jews. He told Nicodemus what he needed to do to enter the kingdom of God.

Jesus said to Nicodemus, *"Most assuredly, I say to you, unless one is born again, he cannot see the kingdom of God."* Nicodemus said to Him, *"How can a man be born when he is old? Can he enter a second time into his mother's womb and be born?"* It is a great question, so Jesus goes on to answer it.

> *"... That which is born of the flesh is flesh, and that which is born of the Spirit is Spirit. Do not marvel that I said to you, you must be born again."*
>
> John 3:3-7.

Our mothers gave birth to us, and we were born into the world as cute little bundles of fleshly babies. But now, we need to experience a spiritual birth and be born again, no matter how old we may be.

Jesus is trying to convince Nicodemus that even though he was a religious leader and had an excellent knowledge of the scriptures, this is no guarantee that he qualifies to enter the kingdom of God. Jesus said, "You must be born again."

Not far from the kingdom

On another occasion, one of the scribes came to Jesus and asked Him,

> *"Which is the first commandment of all?" Jesus answered him. "The first of all commandments is: Hear O Israel, the Lord our God, the Lord is one." And you shall love the Lord your God with all your heart.... "And the second, like it, you shall love your neighbour as yourself. There is no other commandment greater than these."*
>
> Mark 12:28-31.

Jesus told him these were the greatest commandments. The scribe was most impressed by what Jesus said and agreed that loving God and your neighbour is "more than all the burnt offerings and sacrifices."

> *"When Jesus saw he answered wisely, he said to him, "You are not far from the kingdom of God."*
>
> Verse 34.

Not far, meaning close, implying that he still needed to be born again, despite his knowledge and understanding of the scriptures.

I think many religious people today fall into this category. They are not far from entering the kingdom of God. They may have a good knowledge of His word but still need to be born again spiritually.

What will it cost?

Jesus wanted His followers to know that it would cost them. Although the entry fee is free, we are born again and enter the kingdom of God by grace through faith in Christ. Once we become Christians, it becomes a life of total dedication, involving a sacrificial lifestyle as we follow Christ.

Jesus said, *"If anyone desires to come after Me, let Him deny himself, take up his cross daily, and follow Me."* Luke 9:23.

From a Christian perspective, it is harder NOT to take up your cross than to take it up. The devil would have us believe the opposite.

Taking up our cross daily and denying ourselves demands a sacrificial commitment to follow Christ rather than worldly pursuits, but we gain much more in the light of eternity.

We should not look back and long to live according to our old ways. We may be ridiculed for taking a stand to follow Christ and face many temptations to turn back.

"No one, having put his hand to the plow, and looking back, is fit for the kingdom of God."

Luke 9:62.

Once committed to Christ, there is no room for turning back if we are genuine about our allegiance to Christ. It may be easier to follow the crowd, but not so easy to follow Christ.

In his book "The Cost of Discipleship," Dietrich Bonhoeffer says, "When Christ calls a man, he bids him come and die. There are different kinds of dying. It is true, but the essence of discipleship is contained in those words."

Go into all the world

The gospel of the kingdom of God is not just for an exclusive few. It is a message for the whole world.

> *"All authority has been given to Me in heaven and on earth. Go therefore and make disciples of all the nations, baptising them in the name of the Father and of the Son and the Holy Spirit, teaching them to observe all things that I have commanded you; and lo, I am with you always, even to the end of the age."*
>
> Matthew 28:18-20.

Jesus tells us to take this message to the world because all authority has been given to Him, reinforcing His kingship, rule, and supreme authority. But are we clear on what kind of kingdom we proclaim as we go?

Now, and not yet, tension

Author Sarah Bessey quotes, "Sometimes I am so focused on the "not yet" of the kingdom of God that I miss the "now" of it – too."

One of the difficulties of understanding the kingdom of God is the tension between the now and the not yet. The kingdom Jesus inaugurated will eventually become fully realised in the future.

We have already established that His kingdom is not of this world, but for now, in this age, it is spiritual. The Pharisees asked Jesus when the kingdom would come.

> *"The kingdom of God does not come with observation, "nor will they say, "See here" or "See there!" "For indeed, the kingdom of God is within you."*
>
> Luke 17:20-21.

Again, Jesus confirms that it is spiritual and manifests within His people. How does it do this? It is through the supernatural gifts of the Holy Spirit and the evidence of the fruit of the Holy Spirit in our lives. Jesus also spoke of a kingdom still to come. It is an eternal kingdom we enter after death and a kingdom that returns to this earth with Christ.

An unseen dimension

In my last book, "But for the Grace of God Go I," I called the last chapter "Portals of Grace." Just like when we see people in the movies go through a portal that opens up, and they enter a fantasy land or another planet light years away from Earth, I suggested that there are spiritual portals that reveal another dimension.

There is the account of the dying thief on the cross next to Jesus, saying, *"Lord, remember me when you come into your kingdom."* Jesus said to him, *"Today you will be with Me in Paradise."* – Luke 23:42-43.

The dying thief asks to be remembered when he comes into Jesus' kingdom. Death is like going through a portal to another dimension. In this instance, Jesus calls it Paradise.

Other possible portals include Jacob's ladder with angels descending and ascending, Elijah's chariot of fire that whisked him away into heaven, and Elisha's servant opening his eyes to another realm. Jesus appeared with Moses and Elijah on the Mount of Transfiguration. The point is that there is an unseen dimension that is part of the kingdom of God.

Johannes Verkuyl is quoted in "Perspectives on the Christian Movement" as saying, "The coming salvation to which the prophets bore witness came true in Jesus Christ. Salvation has arrived, and therefore, the good news that Jesus proclaims describes a kingdom that has both already come and is yet coming."

Jesus introduced the good news of salvation and the ultimate eternal reign of His kingship and kingdom, beginning here and now and yet to come throughout the eternal ages.

Chapter 5

The parables of the kingdom

Jesus explained the character of the kingdom of God in parables. But do we understand what He is talking about? I think most of us assume we do.

A parable is a simple story. It is recorded in the gospels and was central to Jesus' teaching, conveying profound spiritual truths about God's kingdom. However, sometimes people had trouble interpreting these stories, as the meaning was occasionally vague and needed to be explained.

> *"And with many such parables, He spoke the word to them as they were able to hear it. But without a parable, He did not speak to them. And when they were alone, He explained all things to His disciples."*
>
> Mark 4:333-34.

The Greek word for parable is parabole. It is a compound word meaning literally to cast (bole) alongside (para), hence parable. It is casting a new meaning next to an existing one (a comparison). It is like casting a spiritual meaning alongside something commonplace. It occurs in Matthew, Mark, and Luke. John uses another word, paroimia (something unusual or a dark saying), although paroimia can also refer to a parable.

The parables do not appear in the fourth gospel of John. But what seems to be a simple story may have an unusual, dark, or hidden spiritual meaning camouflaged in the parable.

Jesus spoke in strange and disturbing ways at times, which often offended the religious leaders of the day. To illustrate my point, Jesus addressed a self-righteous, smug group of people who thought they had their act together because of their self-righteous works before God. So, Jesus tells the parable of the Pharisee and the publican, who both went to the temple to pray.

> *"The Pharisee stood and prayed thus with himself. "God, I thank you, I am not like other men – extortioners, unjust, adulterers, or even as this tax collector." "I fast twice a week; I give tithes of all I possess." "And the tax collector standing afar off would not so much as raise his eyes to heaven but beat his breast, saying, "God be merciful to me, a sinner!"*
>
> Luke 18:10-14.

By telling this parable, Jesus conveys to the Pharisees that God is not interested in their prideful list of moral and religious works and how they rate their successful score before God. He is more interested in the tax collector's humility, who acknowledges that he is a sinner and needs help.

Kingdom parables

In Matthew, chapter 13, Jesus speaks of seven parables about the kingdom of God. Each one gives us a glimpse into understanding its character.

Several times, Jesus would say, *"The kingdom of God is like"* Then, He would proceed with a parable to describe it.

The first parable is about the Sower who went forth to scatter and sow seed. There seems to be a three-step sequence to this parable: the parable itself, the disciples asking Jesus questions, and then Jesus interpreting it.

The parable of the Sower –

"Behold a Sower went out to sow. And as he sowed, some fell by the wayside, and the birds came and devoured them. Some fell on stony places, where they did not have much earth, and they immediately sprung up because they had no depth of earth. But when the sun was up, they were scorched, and because they had no root, they withered away. And some fell among thorns, and the thorns sprang up and choked them. But others fell on good ground and yielded a crop; some a hundredfold, some sixty, some thirty. He who has ears, let him hear."

Matthew 13:3-9.

The story seems straightforward, but the disciples were puzzled as to where Jesus was going with it. We are told the disciples came to Him and said,

"Why do you speak to them in parables?" He said to them, *"Because it has been given to you to know the mysteries of the kingdom,*

but to them it has not."

Jesus implies that the time is not yet right, for the people are not ready, but you are. We must remember they were hearing this verbally and did not have it written down to study like we do today.

Then Jesus explained it to them by showing them how people will react differently to the gospel of the kingdom, depending on how they receive it and embrace it, as to whether or not they will survive and go the distance.

However, the seed of the word still needs to be sown; regardless of the response, if we are faithful and patient and continue to sow seed, there will eventually be a fruitful harvest.

The parable of the wheat and the tares –

Jesus tells another parable, which is different but has a similar challenge. The parable itself is, again, a straightforward story.

"The kingdom of heaven is like a man who sowed good seed in the field; but while men slept, his enemy came and sowed tares among the wheat and went his way. But when the grain had sprouted and produced a crop, then the tares also disappeared. So, the servants of the owner came and said to him. Sir, did you not sow good seed in your field? How, then does it have tares? He said to them an enemy had done this.

The servants said to him, do you want us then to go and gather them up? But he said, "No, lest while you gather up the tares, you also uproot the wheat with them. Let both grow together until the harvest, and at the time of harvest, I will say to the reapers, First gather together the tares and bind them in bundles and burn them, but gather the wheat into my barn."

Matthew 13:24-30.

So, again, we see the exact sequence emerging. After Jesus sent the multitude away, the disciples came to Jesus and said, *"Explain to us the parable of the tares in the field."* V37.

The good seeds are the disciples and Christians spread by Jesus throughout the world, proclaiming the gospel.

The weeds are sown by the devil, producing bad people. The two grow together and will be separated come harvest time. In the meantime, God allows the two to grow together.

The servants wanted to get rid of the weeds but had become preoccupied with the problem of evil. Like it or not, this is what the kingdom is like; the two will grow together.

Two Parables of Growth –

The following two parables are about the incredible growth and expansion of the kingdom of God.

Firstly, it is like a mustard seed.

"The kingdom of heaven is like a mustard seed, which a man took and sowed in his field. Which indeed is the least of all the seeds; but when it is grown, it is greater than the herbs and becomes a tree, so that the birds of the air come and nest in its branches."

Matthew 13:31-32.

A mustard seed is the smallest of seeds, so the kingdom of God grows from insignificant and small beginnings to the most significant of trees, becoming a place of refuge.

Secondly, it is like leaven.

"The kingdom of heaven is like leaven, which a woman took and hid in three measures of meal till it was all leavened."

Matthew 13:33.

Again, the kingdom of God is almost hidden and unknown but multiplies until it spreads throughout the world.

Two Parables of Value –

The following two parables speak of the incredible value of the kingdom of God.

Firstly, it is like treasure.

"The kingdom of heaven is like treasure hidden in a field, which a man found and hid; and for joy over it, he goes and sells all that he has and buys that field.

Matthew 13:44.

When the hidden treasure is discovered, the man is so overjoyed that he desperately wants it. So, he sells all he has to buy that field. We cannot buy the kingdom of God, but we are prepared to give up everything when we realise how valuable it is.

Secondly, it is like a pearl

It is likened to the most valuable of all pearls.

"The kingdom of heaven is like a merchant seeking beautiful pearls, who, when he had found one pearl of great price, went and sold all that he had and bought it."

Matthew 13:45-46.

Once again, when one discovers the kingdom of God, it is worth giving up everything. It is of immense value. We cannot buy it; we find it, respond to it, and enter it by grace through faith in Christ.

The parable of the dragnet –

"The kingdom of heaven is like a dragnet that was cast into the sea and gathered some of every kind, which when it was full they drew to shore; and they sat down and gathered the good into vessels, but threw the bad away. So, it will be at the end of the age. The angels will come forth, and separate the wicked from the just, and cast them into the furnace of fire. There will be wailing and gnashing of teeth."

Matthew 13:47-50.

It is similar to the parable of the wheat and the tares. A dragnet gathers everything: the good, the bad, and the ugly.

So, too, the kingdom of God gathers up everything in its path. Notice that Jesus implied fish of every kind, which could also refer to every nation, tribe, and tongue on earth.

Once again, we have the harvest, in which the bad are separated and cast into the fire, and the good is kept. It is up to us to decide how to align ourselves with Christ and His kingdom by faith.

Have you understood?

It is not another parable, but Jesus confronts his disciples with this question concerning the parables of the kingdom.

"Have you understood all these things?" They said to Him, "Yes, Lord." Then He said to them. "Therefore, every scribe instructed concerning the kingdom of heaven is like a householder who brings out of his treasure things new and old."

Matthew 13:51-52.

Yes, they said they understood all these things, but what does Jesus mean when He says every scribe instructed concerning the kingdom of heaven is like a householder who brings out of his treasure things new and old?

It speaks of old and new teachings. According to the old covenants God made with Israel, the scribes knew about the kingdom of God. Still, they must interpret these things in light of Jesus's new teachings to the kingdom. So, they had old and new treasures about the kingdom.

Chapter 6

The Kingdom code of conduct

The New Testament does not provide us with a literal 'code of conduct,' but we have teachings, principles, and guidelines for living (we could say kingdom ethics or lifestyle). However, if we introduce a 'code of conduct,' are we putting people back under the law?

Almost all businesses, companies, schools, and churches have a 'code of conduct.' But how can we have a kingdom 'code of conduct' without becoming legalistic?

Some years ago, a church showing signs of legalism invited me to speak at a long weekend camp. The invitation came with strict instructions to wear a suit and tie, which was required for all speakers. I thought this was a bit over the top for camp meetings. I spoke on the theme of spiritual warfare, and the people loved it, but the pastor became very uncomfortable and agitated. Sometime later, I found out he was not only a legalistic control freak but having an affair at the time.

All games have rules. I enjoy golf, but the club also has a 'code of conduct,' including a dress code. It serves as a set of internal guidelines for the members or employees.

However, can we find a 'code of conduct' that applies to the kingdom of God without becoming legalistic or religious? I believe we can. Jesus gave us one, and we must observe it as we live a blessed life in the kingdom of God.

The Sermon on the Mount

Beginning with the Beatitudes, we have a 'code of conduct' (kingdom ethics) to ensure we are blessed as we follow Christ.

The beatitudes have nothing to do with earning our salvation or entering the kingdom of God. We can only be saved and enter the kingdom of God by grace and faith in Christ. In my last book, ***"But for the GRACE of God Go I,"*** I stressed how we are saved by grace and live by grace as Christians.

However, the Beatitudes are like a 'code of conduct' for Christians who have come out of the world's darkness to live in God's kingdom.

"Blessed" at the beginning of each beatitude conveys that you will be happy and fortunate if you live this way. It is the way Jesus wants his followers to live in His kingdom.

This 'code of conduct' is often the opposite of how the world thinks. We are inclined to gag and say, "Jesus, you cannot be serious." "If I live this way, I will never get anywhere." It is a lifestyle that appears too meek and mild to survive. But that is not what Jesus is saying.

Unlike the world, Christianity is not based on the worldly 'dog eat dog' kind of attitude where you always have to come out on top.

On the other hand, it should not be an excuse for Christians to become lazy and irresponsible. We should still desire to do well and be successful in life.

So, to understand this, let us begin by briefly looking at each beatitude, as listed in Matthew chapter 5, before looking at the rest of the Sermon on the Mount. We may all vary slightly in our interpretations, but this is mine.

"Blessed are the poor in spirit, for theirs is the kingdom of heaven."
– Verse 3.

To be poor in Spirit is to acknowledge that we are spiritually impoverished and in desperate need of God and His forgiveness and are willing to cast ourselves upon God's grace.

"Blessed are those who mourn, for they shall be comforted." – Verse 4.

It speaks of personal loss, mourning a loved one, financial support, employment, and possessions. It is a message of comfort to all who mourn for something and a reassurance that you shall find comfort regardless of your loss.

"Blessed are the meek, for they shall inherit the earth." – Verse 5.

It is not weakness but gentleness. You do not have to be overbearing and oppressive to possess the earth. You can succeed through self-control and gentleness. However, it does not mean you become the devil's doormat. It is having faith, patience, and endurance.

"Blessed are those who hunger and thirst for righteousness, for they shall be filled." – Verse 6

It has to do with justice and honesty. So many people experience injustice. But God is righteous, and those who hunger and thirst for righteousness shall find satisfaction.

"Blessed are the merciful, for they shall obtain mercy." – Verse 7.

We all need mercy. The way to get it is to be merciful. It is like what you sow, you reap. We should not be quick to judge or condemn. If we err, it should be on the side of mercy.

"Blessed are the pure in heart, for they shall see God." – Verse 8.

The core of our being is the condition of the heart. It speaks of having pure motives. It is not deceptive in any way. It is to be open and honest without concealing any dark secrets.

"Blessed are the peacemakers, for they shall be called the sons of God." – Verse 9.

Jesus is called the Prince of Peace. He wants us, as his children, to be ambassadors to bring peace wherever we go. We are to be peacemakers.

"Blessed are those who are persecuted for righteousness sake, for theirs is the kingdom of heaven." – Verse 10.

Those who are persecuted for following Jesus belong to the kingdom of God. Their faith and faithfulness ensure they have eternal life and will always be a part of it.

Conduct contrary to the Beatitudes –

The list is too long to mention all forms of conduct contrary to the Beatitudes.

However, at the time of writing, Domestic violence is a serious issue in Australia. It refers to any form of violence or abuse that is physical, emotional, psychological, financial or sexual between people who are in a domestic or intimate relationship. This is often between spouses or partners, children or other family members. The government is trying to address the issue.

But the real problem is in the heart and mind of the individual who is guilty of such violence. This violates the love of God and demonstrates the need for the kingdom's 'code of conduct' we have been promoting.

A classic Scriptural example of the disciples displaying an unacceptable 'code of conduct' contrary to the Beatitudes is their reaction to the Samaritan village that rejected Christ.

"But they did not receive Him because His face was set for the journey to Jerusalem. When the disciples James and John saw this, they said, Lord, do you want us to command fire to come down from heaven and

consume them, just as Elijah did? But He turned and rebuked them and said, you do not know of what manner of Spirit you are of. For the Son of Man did not come to destroy men's lives but to save them."

Luke 9:53-56.

They became judgmental, wanting to call down fire from heaven and destroy them. They acted in the wrong spirit, certainly not in keeping with the beatitudes or the rest of the sermon on the Mount.

Sermon on the Mount continued

It is a lengthy teaching covering many aspects of kingdom life. Most of it is relatively straightforward and reasonably easy to understand but not easy to implement.

The highlight for me is how Jesus sets the tone by saying that those in the kingdom of God are the salt of the earth and the light of the world.

"You are the salt of the earth, but if the salt loses its flavour, how shall it be seasoned? It is then good for nothing but to be thrown out and trampled underfoot of men." – Verse 13.

I remember an old missionary doctor who lived in a remote area of China describing how salt that had lost its flavour would be thrown onto roads covered in ice and snow to be trampled underfoot.

The implication is that Christians are like preservatives in the world. We should maintain a healthy witness for all to observe. If we lose that witness, we are good for nothing and will not impact our world.

A similar instruction follows it -

"You are the light of the world. A city that set on a hill cannot be hidden. Nor do they light a lamp and put it under a basket, but on a lampstand, and it gives light to all who are in the house. Let your light shine before men that they may see your good works and glorify your Father in heaven." – Verse 14-16.

We, as Christians, shine as lights in a dark world. We are, therefore, encouraged to let our light shine and not go into hiding. We should not hide our light because we are embarrassed by being Christian. We should guide and influence others by letting our light shine.

Some instructions that make us cringe -

Jesus goes on to cover many other aspects of kingdom life, but I will mention three that make most of us cringe.

Turn the other cheek, go the second mile, and love your enemies.

These instructions are so contrary to human nature that they make us cringe. Under the law, you could retaliate (an eye for an eye and a tooth for a tooth).

But Jesus leaves no room for striking back or taking revenge. Turning the other cheek, going the second mile, and loving our enemies seems impossible. Only by the grace of God is this possible. As citizens of the kingdom of God, we are encouraged always to act this way.

Give to him that asks you, and from him who would borrow from you, turn not away.

It is not as easy as it sounds. Who is asking?

We usually hesitate; it depends on who is asking! How reliable are they? Will it be returned broken or in worse condition? In the Western world, we value our possessions and are reluctant to part with them. It was not much of a problem when we were on the mission field in PNG. According to their "one talk system," those from your clan were expected to share regardless of the consequences.

Be perfect as your Father in heaven is perfect.

It is not an invitation to fall into the perfectionist trap, where we strive to be perfect through our self-righteous works; no, it is a goal to imitate Jesus.

Stop worrying –

One of the most challenging yet reassuring parts of the sermon on the mount is Matthew 6:25-34. Five times in this passage, Jesus tells His disciples to stop worrying about the essentials, like food, drink, and clothing.

I find that very difficult, but Jesus reassures us that if we first seek His kingdom, He will take care of those things.

In Conclusion –

Jesus concludes the Sermon on the Mount with a story about a wise man who builds his house on a rock foundation.

"Therefore, whoever hears these sayings of Mine, and does them, I will liken to a wise man who built his house upon the rock: and the rain descended, the floods came, and the winds blew and beat on that house; and it did not fall, for it was on the rock."

Matthew 7:24-25.

Therefore, the sayings of the Sermon on the Mount are an excellent 'code of conduct' that will help us negotiate the storms of life and experience God's blessing.

THE AMBIGUOUS KINGDOM

Chapter 7

The early church and the kingdom

What is the church's relationship to the kingdom? Do they complement one another? Yes, the message of the kingdom of God was central to the early Christian church's beliefs and mission.

The purpose of the church is to spread the message of the kingdom of God to the world. At the moment, this is incomplete since the church stands between Jesus' introduction of the kingdom and the coming kingdom upon His return.

The Christian church is the ekklesia (the called-out ones) in Greek. It is made up of sinners saved by grace who were called out of the kingdom of darkness into the kingdom of God to proclaim and spread the gospel of the kingdom. It is not physical or materialistic. It is a transformation of heart and mind, a way of living by faith in preparation for eternity. As a believer in Christ, you are already a citizen of heaven. It is His reign in our hearts that matters.

I like the way Timothy J. Keller describes it. He says, "The church is a 'pilot plant' of the kingdom of God. It is not simply a collection of individuals who are forgiven. It is a 'royal nation.' (1 Peter 2:9)." "In other words, a counter-culture. The church is to be a new society in which the world can see what family dynamics, business practices, race relations, and all of life can be under the kingship of Jesus Christ. God is out to heal all the effects of sin: psychological, social, and physical."

What a challenge for the church if it is to be a 'pilot plant' of the kingdom of God on earth. A transformed community that lives by the 'code of conduct' we mentioned in the previous chapter. A church that not only proclaims the gospel of the kingdom but also models it for all to see.

However, the Jews were not expecting a church to be a role model for the kingdom. They were not even expecting a church. They expected a Messiah king to deliver them from the oppression of the Roman Empire.

The idea of the Messiah as king was fundamental to Judaism. The Jews were expecting supernatural divine intervention on a cosmic scale. They thought God would send the Messiah to bring judgment on the Roman Empire and establish the throne of David so He could rule and reign from Jerusalem.

Jesus drops a bombshell

"One day, when it was His turn to read the scripture, Jesus stood up in the synagogue and read from the book of Isaiah the prophet".

Isaiah 61:1-2.

It is recorded in Luke 4:18-19 referring to the one who came to preach the gospel to the poor, to heal the brokenhearted, to proclaim liberty to the captives, the recovery of sight to the blind, to set at liberty those oppressed, and to proclaim the acceptable year of the Lord.

Then Jesus drops a bombshell. *"Today, this scripture is fulfilled in your hearing."* Verse 21.

By saying this, He was telling them I am that person; you are looking at Him. I am the one the scripture is referring to. They were stunned and could not believe what they had just heard. But they marvelled at the gracious words that proceeded out of His mouth, and then reality hit them, and they responded by saying, "Is this not Joseph's son?"

It did not take Jesus long to begin fulfilling this scripture by doing all these things the prophet spoke about. It was essentially a demonstration of the kingdom of God ruling over sin, sickness, and the devil. He proclaimed good news, healed the oppressed, showed justice and mercy, forgave sin, and offered salvation and eternal life to whoever would repent and follow Him.

Jesus did not speak much about the church. Paul and the apostles were left to explain the church and its function. However, Jesus did say the church would face demonic opposition.

The church will overcome

Jesus will build His church and make sure nothing will stop it—not even the gates of hell. This implies that the forces of darkness will try, but the church will prevail and overcome this opposition.

> *"...I will build My church, and the gates of Hades shall not prevail against it. And I will give you (the church) the keys of the kingdom."*
>
> Matthew 16:18-19.

Jesus would have spoken prophetically at this stage, as the early church was only in embryo form. However, Jesus was well aware of the spiritual conflict the church would face.

The apostle Paul encourages believers to dress for battle so that they might survive, stand against, and overcome the enemy.

> *"Put on the whole armour of God, that you may be able to stand against the wiles of the devil. For we wrestle not against flesh and blood, but against principalities, against powers, against the rulers of the darkness of this age, against spiritual hosts of wickedness in the heavenly places. Therefore, take up the whole armour of God, that you may be able to withstand in the evil day, and having done all, to stand."*
>
> Ephesians 6:11-13.

Believers need to understand that spiritual warfare becomes part of the package of being a Christian.

> *"For though we walk in the flesh we do not war according to the flesh. For the weapons of our warfare are not carnal but mighty in God for pulling down strongholds."*
>
> 2 Corinthians 10:3

Our spiritual weapons are mighty. The devil would like to stamp out the church because it holds the keys to the kingdom. It is up to the church to use those keys to bring people out of darkness into the light of the gospel.

Jesus gave one more instruction to his disciples before the church came to fruition on the day of Pentecost.

Tarry or wait?

The last instruction Jesus gave His disciples was to tarry (or wait) in Jerusalem.

> *"Behold I send the Promise of the Father upon you, but tarry in the city of Jerusalem until you are endued with power from on high."*
>
> Luke 24:49.

The word tarry comes from the Greek kathizo, which means to sit down, hover, or hang around. In this case, it was to wait for the promise of the Father.

It is precisely what the disciples were doing on the day of Pentecost. They were tarrying or waiting as instructed until they were endured with power from on high. The expression 'power from on high' refers to the baptism in the Holy Spirit. Jesus said,

THE AMBIGUOUS KINGDOM

"You shall receive power when the Holy Spirit has come upon you."

Acts 1:8.

The word power comes from the Greek Dunamis, meaning a dynamic or miraculous supernatural power. It was evidence that Jesus had risen from the dead and sent the Holy Spirit as He had promised. It also convinced people that He was still working with the disciples and the early church, confirming His word with signs and wonders.

In his book "Power Evangelism," John Wimber states, "The early Christians had an openness to the power of the Holy Spirit, which resulted in signs and wonders and church growth. If we want to be like the early church, we must also be open to the Holy Spirit's power."

Jesus said in Acts 1:5, *"You shall be baptised in the Holy Spirit not many days from now."*

That is what happened on the day of Pentecost.

"When the day of Pentecost had fully come, they were all with one accord, in one place…And they were all filled with the Holy Spirit and began to speak with other tongues, as the Spirit gave them utterance."

Acts 2:1-4.

So, this all began as they tarried in Jerusalem, for Jesus wanted to empower them to preach the gospel of the kingdom, beginning at Jerusalem.

"…You shall be witnesses to Me in Jerusalem, and in Judea and

Samaria and to the end of the earth"

Acts 1:8.

The church uses the keys

The church now holds the keys of the kingdom. It became evident on the day of Pentecost when Peter stood up to explain what was happening and preached Christ to the gathered crowd.

"God made this Jesus, whom you crucified, both Lord and Christ." Now, when they heard this, they were cut to the heart and said to Peter and the rest of the apostles, "Men and brethren, what shall we do?"

Acts 2:36-37.

What a dilemma. After hearing that they had crucified the Lord, they probably wondered if God would cut them off from the kingdom; they had been so eagerly looking forward to entering.

How could they make amends? They said, "What shall we do?" Peter answered their questions by using the keys of the kingdom. He said to them -

"Repent and let every one of you be baptised in the name of Jesus Christ for the remission of sins, and you will receive the gift of the Holy Spirit. For the promise is to you, and to your children, and to all afar off, as many as the Lord our God shall call."

Acts 2:38-39.

The keys Peter used were repentance, water baptism, and baptism in the Holy Spirit. As a result, they gladly received the word and were baptised in water, and that day, about 3,000 souls were added to the church. What a great start!

As a new Christian, I wanted to be baptised in the Holy Spirit with the evidence of speaking in other tongues. When I told the pastor, he told me I needed to be baptised in water first because that was the biblical pattern.

However, at the next prayer meeting I attended, as I was praying, I started quietly speaking in tongues, but I did not tell anybody because I thought I had broken the pattern. I could hardly wait to be baptised. When I came out of the water, I spoke in other tongues. However, there is no such hard-and-fast pattern or formula. God is much more flexible than we are. He does things His way and in His timing.

The formation of the early church

The church began to take shape, and certain things happened as people gathered for fellowship.

In Acts 2:42-47, the believers continued in –

(a) The apostle's doctrine

(b) Fellowshipping together

(c) The breaking of bread

(d) Prayers

(e) Signs and wonders by the apostles

(f) Sharing so all essential needs were met

(g) Praising God

As a result, the Lord gave them favour with the people, and those believers saved were added daily to the church. However, it was not long before persecution came to the church in Jerusalem.

> *"At this time a great persecution arose against the church at Jerusalem; and they were all scattered throughout the regions of Judea and Samaria, except the Apostles" "Therefore, those who were scattered went everywhere preaching the word."*
>
> Acts 8:1-4.

As a result, some of the apostles moved out into other areas to help establish churches. As the believers spread, so did the message of the gospel of the kingdom.

The church is relative, but the kingdom is absolute

The church is here to stay but is relative and subject to change. With every succeeding generation, there are changes; the gospel message may be the same, but methods to reach people change. We adapt to communicate the gospel using modern technology as it advances. Therefore, the church is relative and in a state of continual transition.

There is a turnover of people in churches. Pastors, leaders, elders, and deacons are all subject to change, making the church unpredictable.

Therefore, the church is relative, compared to the gospel of the kingdom, which is absolute. God and His kingdom are unchangeable and eternally secure. It is a beautiful alternative to the temporary glitter of the insecure world we live in today.

Dr. Lester Sumrall, in his book, "The Gifts and Ministries of the Holy Spirit," sums up the early church by stating -

"The infant church born in Jerusalem went forth to challenge and defy the entire Roman Empire with all its paganism, sensualism, witchcraft, and military might. Rome eventually fell, but the church marches on." Yes, the church is still marching on.

Chapter 8

Paul explains and expands the kingdom.

Most New Testament references about the kingdom of God focus on Jesus and the kingdom of God in the gospels. However, the apostle Paul explains and expands the kingdom of God in his epistles.

Paul tells us the spiritual dimension of the kingdom is righteousness, peace, and joy in the Holy Spirit (Romans 14:17, which we refer to several times).

However, he highlights the kingdom of God by emphasising the risen and ruling Christ, which places an eschatological exposition on the second coming. His concept of the kingdom of God is undoubtedly centred on the risen and enthroned Christ. He strongly connects this premise to the redemptive work of the cross.

In chapter one of Colossians. He begins with a thankful

attitude, prays for the Colossians, and thanks God that we have been delivered from the power of darkness and transferred into the kingdom of God because of the blood of Christ.

"He has delivered us from the power of darkness and has conveyed us into the kingdom of the Son of His love, in whom we have redemption through His blood."

Colossians 1:13-14.

Paul then explains that all this is because of the risen and enthroned Christ, who has pre-eminence over everything.

"For by Him all things were created that are in heaven and that are on earth, visible and invisible, whether thrones or dominions or principalities or powers. All things were created through Him and for Him. And He is before all things, and in Him all things consist. And He is the head of the body, the church, who is the beginning, the firstborn from the dead, that in all things He may have the pre-eminence."

Colossians 1:16-18.

He has pre-eminence over everything, including "thrones, dominions, principalities and powers.

Paul then links all this to the resurrection and ascension, Christ being *"the firstborn from the dead"* of all who will believe (v.18), in which he goes into great detail explaining his eschatological point of view in 1 Corinthians 15 and 1 and 2 Thessalonians, which we deal with in other sections.

However, I want to focus mainly on Paul and his expansion

of the kingdom of God. He was to become a great exponent of the proclamation of the gospel of the kingdom, embarking on several missionary journeys.

Some scholars estimate that Paul travelled 10,000 miles throughout the Roman Empire to key cities and places like Ephesus, Philippi, Corinth, Athens, and Rome. He preached in homes and synagogues to Jews and Gentiles, to the rich, but more often to people who were poor, desperate, and receptive to the gospel.

His tireless efforts, theological insights, and cultural adaptability played a crucial role in expanding the kingdom of God.

Paul presented the gospel boldly, taking a stand against Jewish upholders of the law who demanded that Christians observe specific requirements of the law, like circumcision. His fearless and bold approach rubbed off on Christians and helped rapidly spread the gospel.

Paul faced a lot of opposition and persecution, mainly from devout Jews. When Paul was in Thessalonica, certain Jews opposed him, and he was sheltered in Jason's house. We read,

> *"Jason has harboured them, and they are all acting contrary to the decrees of Ceaser, "Saying there is another king – Jesus."*

Acts 17:7.

Proclaiming another king, let alone another kingdom other

than Ceaser and the Roman Empire, was a severe offence. So, preaching the gospel of the kingdom was a dangerous occupation.

J. Oswald Sanders said of boldness, "Men and women of caution never advanced the frontiers of the kingdom of God."

It took courage for Christians to advance the kingdom under Jewish law and the hostile environment of the Roman Empire. However, Christians were free from the strict conditions of keeping the law as they separated from their traditions to follow Christ.

If you face opposition, remember your destiny and purpose in life is not based on what is in front of you but on who is inside of you. *"He who is in you is greater than in the world."* – 1 John 4:4.

The book of Acts concludes with Paul preaching the kingdom of God and teaching about Jesus in Rome.

> *"Then Paul dwelt two whole years in his own rented house, and received all who came to him, preaching the kingdom of God and teaching the things which concern the Lord Jesus Christ with all confidence, no one forbidding him."*
>
> Acts 28:30-31.

Paul was in the heart of the Roman Empire, living in Rome toward the end of his life, but let us examine his background, conversion, ministry, and missions.

Paul explains and expands the kingdom.

An impressive background

Paul, or Saul, was a devout Jew and a scholar before his conversion. Let us look at Philippians 3:5-6.

> "...*Circumcised the eighth day, of the stock of Israel, of the tribe of Benjamin, a Hebrew of Hebrews; concerning the law a Pharisee; concerning zeal, persecuting the church; concerning the righteousness which is in the law, blameless.*"

He had an impressive background from a Jewish point of view before his conversion. You can perhaps understand him persecuting the church to defend his Jewish heritage.

He persecuted believers and was also a witness to the stoning death of Stephen.

Ralph Winter and David Hawthorne, in their book "Perspectives on the Christian Movement" state – "Saul (Paul), admittedly, had certain advantages over Palestinian apostles for cross-cultural missions within the Roman Empire. He was raised in Tarsus, a predominantly Gentile city. He spoke not only Hebrew and Aramaic but also Greek and perhaps Latin. He was born a Roman citizen. And his formal training in the Old Testament scriptures under the scholar Gamaliel enabled him to delineate the Old Testament moorings of Christian faith with unparalleled clarity and precision."

But by the grace of God, the Lord had other plans for his life. He was on his way to the High Priest to seek letters from him to continue to persecute Christians when God apprehended him. When he came near Damascus, a light shone around him from heaven, and he was knocked to the ground and heard a voice saying to him,

"Saul, Saul, why are you persecuting Me?" and he said, *"Who are you, Lord?"* And the Lord said, *"I am Jesus, whom you are persecuting. It is hard for you to kick against the goads."* So, he, trembling and astonished, said, *"Lord, what do you want me to do?"* And the Lord said to him, *"Arise, go into the city, and you will be told what you must do."* – Acts 9:1-6.

Not only was Saul (Paul) converted and became a Christian, but he immediately obeyed the Lord and made himself available to serve.

His purpose and ministry

God had called Paul (Saul) to preach the gospel of the kingdom to the Gentiles.

"I have appeared to you for this purpose to make you a minister… I will deliver you from the Jewish people, as well as from the Gentiles, to whom I now send you, to open their eyes and turn them from darkness to light, and from the power of Satan to God, that they may receive forgiveness of sins and an inheritance among those who are sanctified by faith in Me."

Acts 26:16-18.

The first book I wrote, **"Unlocking Your Purpose,"** was about keys to unlocking your purpose in life. It is something close to my heart.

I do not believe God saves us to keep a seat warm in church

every Sunday. While that may be a good start, God has a plan for your life. Sometimes, we know what it is, or God may unfold it over time.

I did not doubt that God had a purpose for me. What about you? I felt called to the ministry from the moment I was born again, and prophetic words confirmed this throughout my life.

Years before, I was saved and had not even thought about ministry. I remember my mother saying, "Terry, I think you will end up in the ministry." I do not know what made her say that because I was not religious. My mother was a God-fearing person but rarely went to church. Maybe it was prophetic, and she did not realise it then.

Around this time, I met and married my lovely wife, Caroline. After a one-week honeymoon, we spent the first two years of our marriage attending a Bible College in Adelaide in preparation for ministry. The rest is history.

So, we see Paul knew what his calling was. He was to take the gospel to the Gentiles.

> *"For I speak to you Gentiles; in as much as I am an apostle to the Gentiles."*
>
> Romans 11:13.

His Missionary Journeys

Barnabas had been sent from Jerusalem to Antioch to help establish the church. After being in Antioch for a while,

Barnabas travelled to Tarsus to find Saul (Paul) and recruited him to come and help him in Antioch.

Barnabas and Paul formed a team for their first Missionary journey from Antioch. They had a young man named John Mark travel with them. However, John Mark eventually abandoned them, leading to a severe dispute between Barnabas and Paul. Barnabas wanted to restore him, but Paul was reluctant.

There are three significant missionary journeys mentioned in the Book of Acts. The fourth one is unclear, but he ends up in Rome. The message of the gospel of the kingdom through these missionary journeys was the catalyst for its spread to the then-known world and beyond despite persecution and opposition.

I will list a brief outline of their travels.

The **first** missionary journey – They went through Cyprus, Pamphylia, and Galatia.

The **second** missionary journey – They went through Galatia, Macedonia, and Achaia.

The **third** missionary journey – Through Galatia, Asia, Macedonia, and Achaia- ended in Jerusalem.

The **fourth** missionary journey Is unclear but may have included Spain, Crete, Asia, Achaia, and Macedonia. But Paul ended up in Rome.

Some points of interest

Paul explains and expands the kingdom.

A name change –

Before becoming a Christian, he was called Saul of Tarsus. The writer of the book of Acts (Luke) begins to refer to Saul as Paul. He went by both names for many years. The Gentiles would have referred to him by the Greek name Paul, which seems to stick with him for the rest of his life.

"Then Saul, who is also called Paul." – Acts 13:9." He later refers to himself as Paul, an apostle.

The pattern for proclamation –

On all of their journeys, they often used the local synagogue as a platform to preach the gospel.

"And when they arrived in Salamis, they preached the word of God in the synagogues of the Jews."

Acts 13:5.

So, we can understand why most of their opposition came from unbelieving Jews who stirred up trouble. Despite this, they spoke the word boldly, and the Lord confirmed His word with signs and wonders in many places. (Acts 14:3).

The message the apostles proclaimed –

The apostles preached the word of the Lord. *"And the word of the Lord was preached in the region."* – Acts 13:49.

In his book "Preaching and Preachers" Martin Lloyd-Jones says, "The primary task of the church and of the Christian minister is the preaching of the word of God."

We must also assume from Acts 14:22 that preaching the gospel included mentioning the opposition they faced as Christians: "We must, through many tribulations, enter the kingdom of God."

Was it the first Bible School? –

After several months of teaching in the synagogue at Ephesus, possibly due to opposition from some Jews, Paul moved his disciples to the school of Tyrannus. There is some speculation as to what sort of school it was. It could have taught the scriptures, philosophy, or both.

> *"Paul withdrew the disciples, reasoning daily in the school of Tyrannus. And this continued for two years so that all who dwelt in Asia heard the word of the Lord Jesus, both Jews and Greeks."*
>
> Acts 19:9-10.

Tyrannus was in charge, but Paul was allowed to use it for his disciples, and he taught there daily for two years. Maybe the students combined to make it the first bible school in the New Testament.

I know how influential a Bible School can be in an area. When we established a Bible School in Port Moresby, PNG, it impacted the nation and influenced the spread of the gospel for many years.

The Gospel in Rome –

Paul explains and expands the kingdom.

We end the missionary journeys with Paul proclaiming the gospel of the kingdom in Rome.

"I am ready to preach the gospel to you who are in Rome also. For I am not ashamed of the gospel of Christ, for it is the power of God unto salvation for everyone who believes, for the Jew first and also for the Greek" "The just shall live by faith." – Romans 1:15-18. We also read how this happened. *"Paul dwelt two whole years in his own rented house preaching the gospel of the kingdom and teaching about the Lord Jesus Christ with all confidence, no one forbidding him."* – Acts 28:30-31.

In conclusion, the central theme of these missionary journeys revolved around Jesus, the establishment of churches, and the proclamation of the kingdom of God. Paul also wrote Epistles with incredible theological insights into understanding the word of God. He engaged with different cultures and endured persecution and adversity to expand the gospel of the kingdom.

We all have a part to play

Every church member has a role in spreading the gospel. We can do this through our church, homes, workplace, community, family, friends, and relatives.

We need to be actively involved in spreading the gospel of the kingdom at whatever level we have the opportunity to do so. If we do, we will be blessed and be a blessing to others.

THE AMBIGUOUS KINGDOM

Chapter 9

The substance of the kingdom

The substance of the kingdom of God explores the inner realities of our relationship with God. It transforms our lives, shapes our faith, gives us a purpose for our existence, and an eternal perspective on life.

A quote by theologian Os Guinness states –

"Jesus made clear that the kingdom of God is organic and not organisational. It grows like a seed and works like leaven: secretly, invisibly, surprisingly, and irresistibly."

By organic, he refers to that which is from living matter. It refers to the spiritual substance of the kingdom, which is hard to figure out from a natural or worldly point of view.

Substance is an interesting word that we use for various purposes. We may say someone has substance or lacks substance. It is usually an assessment referring to the depth of their character, knowledge, ideas, and actions or the lack of those things.

A more literal meaning is found in Luke 8:3, where certain women, Mary Magdalene, Joanna, Susanna, and many others, provided for Jesus from their substance, mainly food and other essential provisions.

The dictionary defines substance as "The real or essential part or element of anything; essence, reality, or basic matter. The physical matter of which a thing consists." How do we apply this to the kingdom of God?

Spiritual substance?

If the kingdom of God consists of spiritual substance, can we begin to define that substance? I feel like the proverbial dog chasing its tail, trying to come to grips with the substance of the kingdom. But trust me; we are making some headway. But let me now stretch your thinking by giving you something to explore -

Science and Quantum Physics -

I do not pretend to understand it, but Science has always told us that nothing exists out there but space. However, Quantum Physics and Quantum Mechanics tell us there is no such thing as empty space. They now tell us there is an energy and a source that we cannot see, giving rise to everything material that we do see throughout the universe, and this energy holds everything together. Jesus could not use this terminology in His day on earth, but maybe when Jesus refers to the kingdom of God, it includes this dimension Quantum science is now discovering. Several books have been published lately exploring these possibilities.

Anyway, the above theory reminds me of some scriptures I will refer to below and interpret in a more traditional manner.

> *"Now faith is the substance of things hoped for the evidence of things not seen" "By faith we understand that the worlds were framed by the word of God so that things which are seen were not made of things which are visible."*

Hebrews 11:1-3.

Faith is the substance of things hoped for, including the things we cannot yet see. The Greek word for substance *hypostasis* in this scripture means 'that which stands under' or 'supports.' So, Paul is saying that faith undergirds or supports what we hope for. This is a faith based on the word of God.

> *"So, then faith comes by hearing and hearing by the word of God."*

Romans 10:17.

The word of God framed the world. If we go back to creation in the beginning (Genesis 1:1-3), we have the Word and the Spirit working together at the time of creation, making the invisible visible.

We have already established that the gospel of the kingdom is spiritual here and now and that it is not of the kingdoms of this world. So, the kingdom of God is spiritual and undergirded by our faith in the Word and the Spirit, which gives it substance.

The epistles confirm and highlight this thought from a theological point of view, giving us a greater understanding of the kingdom's substance.

We learn more about the substance of the kingdom by examining Romans 14:17.

> *"For the kingdom of God is not eating and drinking, but righteousness and peace and joy in the Holy Spirit."*
>
> Romans 14: 17.

We must remember this is in the context of what food is acceptable for Christians and what is not. The issue is that it does not matter much; it depends on your faith as to what you eat and do not eat. According to scripture, Christians can sanctify food through the prayer of faith.

The fundamental insight into this scripture is that the substance of the kingdom of God is righteousness, peace, and joy in the Holy Spirit.

In this context, it implies that we should not let food destroy these spiritual qualities, especially our love for one another and our fellowship over disputes about food.

When I go to McDonalds with my son-in-law Carl (who has designed all my books), he orders extra pickles, but I order no pickles. There is no dispute over which is best (although Carl assures me Jesus would have preferred pickles). It is a matter of personal preference and has nothing to do with the kingdom of God (as long as we sanctify it by faith).

In his book "The Gospel of the Kingdom," George Eldon Ladd says, "Righteousness, peace, and joy are the fruits of the Spirit which God bestows now upon those who yield their lives to the rule of the Spirit."

So, we could say these spiritual qualities are holy, pure, and everlasting substances of the kingdom of God. Like food, they are not subject to corruption, decay, or time. These spiritual qualities are of immense value and worth protecting.

Verse 18 is like a conclusion to verse 17. *"For he who serves Christ in these things (righteousness, peace, and joy) is acceptable to God and approved by men."*

We have physical limitations

We like to keep ourselves in shape.

But Paul cautions Timothy by telling him to –

"Reject profane and old wives fables, and exercise yourself toward godliness. For bodily exercise profits a little, but godliness is profitable for all things, having promise of the life that now is and of that which is to come."

1 Timothy 4:7-8.

Paul is not knocking exercise or bodily strength; he is reminding Timothy of what should be his priority in ministry. Although it is wise to try and keep ourselves in shape, Godliness is more profitable in this life and what is to come (eternity). He should stick to things that pertain to the kingdom of God.

Paul would instead demonstrate God's strength and power through his gospel presentation. Paul writes to the Corinthians, saying -

"I was with you in weakness, in fear, and in much trembling. And my speech and my preaching were not with persuasive words of human wisdom, but in demonstration of the Spirit and of power, that your faith should not be in the wisdom of men but in the power of God."

1 Corinthians 2:3-5.

Paul is not trying to impress anyone with his human wisdom and words; he is intent on demonstrating the kingdom of God through the power of the Holy Spirit. He wants people to put their faith in the reality of God's power.

Again, in I Corinthians 4:20, *"For the kingdom of God is not in word but in power."*

Demonstrating kingdom power

The obvious question is, how was this power being demonstrated? Paul implies that the Gentiles were convinced by -

"...mighty signs and wonders, by the power of the Holy Spirit of God, so that from Jerusalem and round about to Illyricum I have fully preached the gospel of Christ"

Romans 15, 18-19.

Paul says, *"I have fully preached the gospel."* What does it mean to preach the gospel fully? It means he preaches all

The substance of the kingdom

of it, including the ministry of signs and wonders, by the power of the Holy Spirit. He does not avoid certain aspects of the gospel like some are inclined to do today. Only by preaching the gospel fully could the preacher and the hearer be completely satisfied.

The term 'full gospel' includes signs and wonders and many other issues too numerous to mention, including the nitty-gritty areas relevant to church discipline and the gospel of the kingdom.

But again, Paul emphasises how God confirmed His word with the following signs:

> *"God also bearing witness both with signs and wonders, with various miracles, and gifts of the Holy Spirit, according to His own will."*
>
> Hebrews 4:2.

As believers, living in the dimension of this power makes signs, wonders, and miracles available. It demonstrates to humanity that God is concerned for our well-being and health if we are prepared to put our faith in Christ.

E. Stanley Jones, in his book The Unshakable Kingdom and the Unchanging Person, describes it this way: "Jesus radiated health, and He cured disease by His command and touch. He was the holiest, healthiest, and healingest person who ever lived. Just being in His presence is healing. They found healing by living in the holiest, healthiest, and healingest order that ever existed—the Kingdom of God."

Our spiritual inheritance

Who qualifies for an inheritance in the kingdom of God? All believers do. What will that look like?

Both my wife and I received an inheritance from our parents when they passed away. We qualified because we were their children. It is no different in the kingdom of God. We qualify because we are His children and citizens of the kingdom of God.

How do we become children of God? We must be born again to enter the kingdom. It is by a spiritual birth. It does not depend upon our status in society, nationality, education, or any other qualification we may obtain in life.

> *"Now this I say, that flesh and blood will not inherit the kingdom of God; nor does corruption inherit incorruption."*
>
> 1 Corinthians 15:50.

However, the kingdom of God is both a present spiritual reality and yet to be bestowed upon believers at the return of Christ.

> *"When the Son of Man comes in His glory, and all the Holy angels with Him, then He will sit on the throne of His glory… "Then the King will say to those on His right hand, Come, you blessed of My Father, inherit the kingdom prepared for you from the foundation of the world."*
>
> Matthew 25:31-34.

Rewards for service

Scripture tells us there are rewards for proclaiming the gospel of the kingdom, both here and now and in the kingdom yet to come. Most of the rewards now relate to financial and material rewards and, of course, the blessing of God in different ways.

In her book "Tentmakers Needed for World Evangelism." Ruth E. Siemens expounds on why the apostle Paul worked as a tentmaker.

She commends Paul for his tent-making skills and for handling the overall financial requirements for his ministry. She lists the three reasons Paul continued his secular work under these headings: "Credibility, Identification, and Modelling." Although Paul sometimes worked to help support himself, the gospel preacher is entitled to be supported by the gospel. What about rewards yet to come? Yes, everyone who labours in the gospel will receive a reward.

"Each one will receive his own reward according to his own labour."

1 Corinthians 3:8.

Shepherds who shepherd God's flock will receive a crown of glory as their reward. – (1 Peter 5:4).

"Shepherd the flock of God which is among you. When the Chief Shepherd appears, you will receive the crown of glory that does not fade away."

We are also warned to guard against those trying to deprive us of some of our rewards.

"For many deceivers have gone out into the world who do not confess Jesus Christ as coming in the flesh. This is a deceiver and an anti-Christ. Look to yourselves that we do not lose those things we worked for but that we may receive a full reward."

2 John 7-8.

Serving God in His kingdom is not a thankless task. Labouring for the gospel's sake with the promise of rewards is an incentive to be faithful and endure hardships as soldiers of Christ, knowing that one day we will be rewarded. – (2 Timothy 2:3).

But we need to remind ourselves that we are not striving in our strength. We are doing it by the power of the Holy Spirit.

"Not by might nor by power but by My Spirit, Says the Lord of hosts."

Zechariah 4:6.

Chapter 10

Is the Kingdom relevant for us today?

Christians view the kingdom of God as a present reality central to their belief system. Even if they do not understand everything, this gives them hope for the future. But how relevant is the kingdom of God for us in our modern world today?

Jesus introduced the message of the gospel of the kingdom of God some two thousand years ago. The early church and subsequent churches have proclaimed it to this day, so it is still relevant. But do we understand it?

The Oxford Dictionary defines 'relevance' as 'closely connected or appropriate to what is being done or considered.'

So, we must consider our connection with what is being done or discussed concerning the kingdom of God and its relevance to our modern world.

Many things posted on Facebook are relevant to me, and I connect with them. On the other hand, there are many irrelevant things, so I disconnect from them by ignoring or deleting them.

Is the kingdom of God relevant to everybody everywhere? Is there such a thing as total relevancy?

Most things in life are temporary and are only relevant for a time and a season.

"To everything, there is a season, a time for every purpose under heaven."

Ecclesiastes 3:1.

For example, a particular school you attended is relevant to you for a limited time. It also applies to where we live, our house, church, job, family, car, and possessions; these are all relevant for a time and a season.

Relevant to all of us

There is only one thing relevant to all of us, everywhere, in every situation, at all times, and that is the kingdom of God. Everyone is under the influence of the kingdom of God, even though they may be oblivious to it. They will either be ignorant of it, rebelling against it, or submitting to it.

When Jesus was asked by the Pharisees when the kingdom of God would come, He answered them and said, –

"The kingdom of God does not come with observation; nor will they

say, "See here!" or "See there!" For indeed, the kingdom of God is within you."

Luke 17:20 -21.

When Jesus said the kingdom of God is within you, was He referring to His presence within their midst, or was he referring to the kingdom inside them? How could the kingdom be inside a Pharisee when he is not born again? What could this mean?

The rules and laws of the kingdom affect the whole of creation. However, most people are not aware of it. Therefore, it is relevant to everybody, even to those who are not yet born into it.

So, in theory, no other relevance exists. It sounds like a contradiction: we are all subject to the kingdom of God but not citizens of it until we are born again.

Jesus told Nicodemus, a religious leader and a Pharisee, *"Most assuredly, I say to you unless one is born of water and the Spirit again, he cannot enter the kingdom of God."* – John 3:5.

He explains that it is a spiritual birth that enables him to see and enter the kingdom.

The implication is that the kingdom is already among us. Still, we are not subject to it, or do we comprehend it until our eyes open to this spiritual dimension by being born again. We are then challenged to live according to God's will in the kingdom of God.

Coming out of darkness

By being born again, it is as though someone has turned on a light, and the kingdom of God suddenly becomes relevant to us. It is the process of coming out of the kingdom of darkness into the kingdom of His dear Son, a kingdom of light.

> *"For He rescued us from the kingdom of darkness and transferred us into the kingdom of His dear Son, who purchased our freedom and forgave our sins."*
>
> Colossians 1:13-14. (NLT).

We do not realise that we have been living in darkness under the god (the devil) of this world system. But now we are transferred out of that darkness into His glorious light. It is as though a whole new dimension of the Spirit has opened up to us. We now have the task of learning to walk in the Spirit, which is challenging for all Christians.

The teachings of Jesus

Now, we begin to see the teachings of Jesus take on a new dimension for us.

The Beatitudes and the rest of the Sermon on the Mount seem so contrary to worldly ways, but now we see why this kingdom's 'code of conduct' we looked at in chapter six is so different from the ways of the world.

Remember how Jesus is telling us how to react to our enemies. Love your enemies! Are you kidding? It seems impossible to a worldly person and very difficult for a

Christian, but Jesus does not mock us and expects us to adapt to these kingdom principles. What a different world we would live in if everyone practised this.

The Royal Law of Love

James uses this principle to address an issue of inequality that had crept into the church. He applies what he calls the "Royal Law."

> *"If you really fulfill the Royal Law according to the scripture, "You shall love your neighbour as yourself." You do well, but if you show partiality, you commit sin and are convicted by the law as transgressors. For whoever shall keep the whole law and yet stumble i n one point, he is guilty of all."*
>
> James 2:8-10.

The issue they faced in the church was partiality. When a rich man came into the church, he was ushered to a good seat and treated better than the poor man who went into the church.

> *"For if there should come into your assembly a man with gold rings and fine apparel, and there should also come in a poor man in filthy clothes, and you pay attention to the one wearing fine clothes and say to him, "You sit here in a good place," and say to the poor man, "You stand there" or "Sit here at my footstool," have you not shown partiality among yourselves, and have become judges with evil thoughts?"*
>
> James 2:2-4.

We would not be human if we did not succumb to this

temptation at times. As a pastor, I have had wealthy people in the church make substantial financial donations, for which I was very grateful at the time. The temptation is to honour them above others, but this violates the Royal Law of Love. We are all equal in the kingdom of God. God wants us to be careful not to neglect the poor and needy.

While on the mission field, our home church in Australia withdrew our support because I said we would only be away for twelve months. But then I decided we needed another two years to accomplish our mission (which ended up as another five), so they withdrew our support.

We were devastated, but a couple of widows in that church sent us regular donations to tide us over until another church in Australia took up our support.

It was not the wealthy who would have had a surplus God used; it was a couple of widows. From our point of view, they were hearing from the Lord as we were desperate at the time. The fact is we never know how God will provide.

Christianity is a unique lifestyle

In our modern world, true Christianity is a unique and different lifestyle. We are under immense pressure to conform to worldly standards that erode morality.

I will mention a few challenges we face today.

Moral relevance -

Today, the church faces many moral issues that are

becoming more acceptable in our social structure.

The Gay and Lesbian influence raises the issue of same-sex marriage, as opposed to the biblical sanctity of marriage. Also, other moral problems that date back to the bible days. Paul addresses a similar problem with Christians living in the immoral Roman culture. Which in many ways would have been identical to ours today.

"…. Present your bodies a living sacrifice, holy, acceptable to God, which is your reasonable service. And do not be conformed to this world, but be transformed by the renewing of your mind…"

Romans 12:1-2.

It is a battle we face when we become Christians. We have turned away from our old ways and no longer want to conform to this world.

We now desire to live according to a kingdom's 'code of conduct' that is contrary to the immoral standards of this world. Many people today are determined to do their own thing.

In their book "The Gospel in the Modern World," Martyn Eden and David F. Wells say, "So the insistence of the scriptures that God Himself has acted in history, and thereby constituted oral criteria for human action in history, is a major feature of biblical ethics. This sets it against the hyper-individualism of existentialism, in which every individual must re-invent the moral wheel for himself in each moment of decision, and the hyper-corporation of New Age superconsciousness, which virtually dissolves personal morality, as most pantheisms ultimately do."

That sums up our modern world today. Everyone is reinventing the moral wheel to suit themselves instead of turning to the Bible for guidance.

Cultural relevance -

You probably ask questions like, what about allowing for different cultural influences?

Although we live in a multicultural world, the gospel of the kingdom is still relevant in every culture. We need to be tolerant and considerate of different cultures and not assume that any culture (mainly Western) is superior to any other culture. Sometimes, missionaries, in particular, felt that any culture other than Western was somewhat sinful and inferior and should be changed. However, there may be more significant challenges with some cultures than others.

While on the mission field in PNG, we found witchcraft and sorcery were interwoven into the culture. However, the gospel of the kingdom is cross-cultural and multi-cultural and is relevant to all cultures.

> *"This gospel of the kingdom will be preached in all the world as a witness to all the nations, and then the end will come."*
>
> Matthew 24:14.

Atonement relevance -

In this modern world, there is a tendency to question the relevance of the atonement for sin. On the basis that sacrifices are a thing of the past and are no longer required. What some fail to see is that Christ put an end to sacrifices by becoming the last sacrifice, as the sacrificial Lamb of God.

> *"And according to the law, almost all things are purified with blood, and without the shedding of blood, there is no remission." "For it is impossible that the blood of bulls and goats could take away sins." "We have been sanctified through the offering of the body of Jesus Christ once for all."*
>
> Hebrews 9:22, 10:4, and 10.

Therefore, the atonement revealed in scripture must remain at the centre of the gospel message.

Even though much of the gospel has its roots in the typology of the Old Testament, once understood in the light of the New Testament, we can see just how relevant the atonement for sin is for us today.

THE AMBIGUOUS KINGDOM

Chapter 11

The kingdom and modernity

The relationship between the kingdom of God and modernity is complex and depends upon how we view it. Some aspects of modernity, such as secularism, individualism, and materialism, may conflict with kingdom values that emphasise spirituality, community, and selflessness.

The principles of the kingdom of God can be relevant within modern contexts, adhering to social justice, compassion, and ethical living. So, it depends on our perspective and interpretation of both concepts.

The kingdom of God intersects with various aspects of modernity. It can inspire individuals and communities to work towards a world characterised by justice, peace, and love through Christ in this modern age.

The root of modernity is from the Latin word *modernus*, meaning 'modern.' It is the quality of being current or of the present. It follows on from the previous chapter on relevancy.

If we were to use modernity conversationally, we could say, "This city has been too old-fashioned and traditional for too long. We could put a new shopping centre in the heart of it that would instil a spirit of modernity in this area."

Is the kingdom of God too old-fashioned and traditional for this modern world we live in today?

This is not an attempt to study modernity but how we remain faithful as Christians to the kingdom of God under the pressure of modernity. How can we translate the gospel in palatable terms in this modern world?

What modernity looks like

Modernity is a constellation of many forces working together to create a modern world. Some of these are –

(a) Globalisation

The world is continually moving toward Globalisation. There are advantages and disadvantages. We could make a list of positives and negatives. Whatever happens in one part of the world may affect the rest. Global communication brings the world into our lounge rooms. Some would like to see a world government controlling an international environment, economy, and religion. This could be very dangerous if the wrong people are in charge. It is something the Anti-Christ would be more than happy to control.

(b) Ideologies

Several ideologies have emerged, such as capitalism, socialism, liberalism, communism, and modernism. These ideologies, on their own, are struggling to survive. Some may have to compromise and merge to bring about an effective solution for stability in the world. None of these can ever be a substitute for the kingdom of God.

(c) Knowledge

There is worldwide pressure to increase knowledge to the advantage of whoever has it. We have made tremendous headway with improved health systems. But we have also seen the devastating effects of modern warfare. Nuclear weapons threaten the world's survival. We race to explore space to the advantage of those who are able. Knowledge has given us a computerised world, including the mobile phone, which has transformed our way of living.

(d) Urbanisation

There is a tendency for people to drift in population from rural areas to the cities. The cities provide the infrastructure and modern facilities that people need today. It may appear unifying, but it is fragmenting much of society. Our quest for bigger, better, and faster has eroded traditional values, which were once a community's fabric.

(e) Secularism

Secularism is a philosophy that holds no religious commitment at all. The likes of agnostics, communists, and atheists are increasing in this modern world. Christianity is also spreading rapidly in some areas. Secularism still has a stronghold on the world and is becoming more prevalent.

(f) Modern Consciousness

Modern consciousness encompasses practical methodology that leverages and uniquely combines existing and emerging disciplines and practices in multiple fields to expand our perception beyond our worldview, which is deeply rooted in beliefs, thoughts, and emotions we have habituated in the past. This is more in line with new-age thinking, which gives you the freedom to be and love yourself according to your consciousness.

Taking opportunities to share our faith -

We still need to share our faith despite the influences of modernity. I want to take a moment to share a recent experience I had with someone who was influenced by a secular worldview. While writing my second book, "Enjoying Your Twilight Years," I struck up a friendship with a man named John, who was around my age. Most mornings, I would buy a drive-thru Maccas breakfast and go by the river to pray and eat (mainly). John would walk past with his dog every morning and stop, and we would chat casually.

One morning, I went to start my car, and the battery was flat. I was about to call the RACQ for help but had forgotten my mobile phone. But John gave me his phone so I could call for help. I felt the Lord prompted me to put the incident in the book and mention John. So I did, thinking it had little relevance to the book.

After publishing the book, I gave John a copy and told him he was in it. He was thrilled but a bit stunned when he saw the Christian content. He said, "My wife does not believe in anything, and I am unsure what I think." The last few chapters were about preparing for heaven. John read it, and when he went past, he would stop and tell me where he was up to and how good it was. The last time I saw him, he thanked me for the book and said he had passed it on to his sister. A few months went by, and I had not seen John. I thought it was strange, so I asked someone I had seen him walk with about what had happened to John. I was shocked when he said John had passed away in his sleep a few months ago.

I feel that I will meet John in heaven, and he will thank me for introducing him to Jesus.

Is modernity the real problem?

Modernity may present some problems concerning the kingdom of God, but I think modernity has tremendous advantages for us in our modern world.

We have already mentioned a number, but advances in medical science, technology, and communication have completely changed our lifestyle for the better.

The first car I had was an old hotted-up FJ Holden. It was a lot of fun, but I would hate to be still driving it today. It had no safety features like the basic seat belts, airbags, and power steering we have as standard car equipment today. I currently drive a Rav 4 Toyota Hybrid loaded with safety features.

I was raised in the country and remember ice chests before refrigerators, scrubbing boards before washing machines, wood stoves before electric hotplates, kettles, electric jugs, and microwaves. I would not want to return to the so-called good old days.

So, what is the real problem?

Modernity may be facing some problems. But why does Christianity sometimes clash with modernity?

The world already opposes the gospel of the kingdom, which causes conflict for Christians trying to communicate the gospel in their community.

> *"I have given them your word, and the world has hated them because they are not of the world, just as I am not of the world."*
>
> John 17:14.

It is not so much modernity that is the major problem. It was not an issue in the days Jesus ministered on earth. But Jesus and Christians have always faced opposition from the world.

So, what is the real issue? It is the antichrist spirit in the world fuelled by the god of this world, the devil, that is the real problem.

> *"But even if our gospel is veiled, it is veiled to those who are perishing, whose minds the god of this age has blinded, who do not believe, lest the light of the gospel of the glory of Christ, who is the image of God, should shine on them."*
>
> 2 Corinthians 4:4.

Regarding the above scripture, I was preaching in a meeting in PNG, and when I gave an altar call for people to receive Christ, a man started to yell out, "Help me, I have gone blind." We prayed for him, and God restored his sight. We later found out that he practised sorcery and came to disrupt the meeting. So, whatever the devil intended to do backfired, and he immediately came to faith in Christ.

The devil is doing all he can to discredit Christ and Christianity. It is an antichrist spirit. As the name suggests, it is against Christ.

> *"Every spirit that does not confess that Jesus Christ has come in the flesh is not of God. And this is the spirit of the antichrist, which you have heard was coming and is now already in the world."*
>
> 1 John 4:3.

Although modernity may have some challenges for Christians, our real war is against the evil in this world system instigated by the devil and the antichrist spirit infiltrating the world.

THE AMBIGUOUS KINGDOM

Chapter 12

The kingdom is a word in season

A 'word in season' refers to something timely or appropriate for a particular situation, time, and place. As I look back and reflect on my time in ministry, I realise I was more of a seasonal preacher. I liked to speak on topics appropriate to the times and seasons we seem to be experiencing. I would also like to take a series on various subjects.

"A man has joy by the answer of his mouth and a word spoken in due season; how good it is!"

Proverbs 15:23.

A word in due season is a good word that can minister to people in a relevant way. It is easy for them to understand and apply. All preachers have different styles, and no matter how they vary in how and what they preach, one subject is always seasonal: the gospel of the kingdom.

Paul writes to Timothy, saying – *"I charge you, therefore, before God and the Lord Jesus Christ, who will judge the living and the dead at His appearing and His kingdom: Preach the word! Be ready in season and out of season. Convince, rebuke, exhort, with all longsuffering and teaching."* – 2 Timothy 4:2.

He is telling Timothy to preach the word in and out of season. Not focusing on circumstances or results, good or bad, but on preaching the word. He is to take his ministry seriously because one day, he will have to give an account of his ministry before God in His coming kingdom.

So, Preach the word in the season as you have exceptional opportunities or out of season when things are tough and opportunities are few.

He warns Timothy that the days are coming when some will not endure sound doctrine. I would suggest that the kingdom of God is always a sound subject we can communicate regardless of the season.

I will never forget attending a conference many years ago when I heard E. V. Hill preaching from Acts 8 on how Philip, during a time of persecution, went down to the city of Samaria and preached 'Christ,' and a revival broke out. His message was, "Preach Christ, for He is preachable." So, despite the season you may be in; Christ and His kingdom is always preachable.

Communication skills

All Christians, especially church leaders, preachers, and

teachers, should always strive to improve their communication skills. Communicating the gospel of the kingdom is a continual challenge.

James J. Murphy, in his book, "Augustine and the Debate about Christian Rhetoric," quotes Augustine as saying, "There are two things necessary to the treatment of scripture: A way of discovering 'modus inveniendi' those things which are to be understood, and a way of expressing to others 'modus proferendi' what we have learned."

Yes, it is one thing to discover and understand the things we have learned, but another to express them clearly.

(a) Use your words

Words are unique to the human race. God created man in His image and communicated with him through language using words. We had a grandson who was beginning to stammer and showing signs of stuttering. Our daughter would gently tell him to slow down and say, "Now, choose and use your words."

My wife and I sometimes have to tell young people who often talk so fast to slow down so we can understand them. But then maybe we are just showing our age.

If we are trying to communicate the gospel of the kingdom, we need to consider who we are talking to so we can adjust how we express our message.

(b) Finding common ground

When communicating the gospel, looking for common ground is a good idea. 'Communication' comes from the Latin word 'communis,' which means 'common.' It is easy to communicate if "commonness" can be established. Let me share a few examples. As fishermen, Jesus said to Simon Peter and his brother Andrew, *"Follow me, and I will make you fishers of men."* – Matthew 4:19.

He said to the women at the well, *"If you knew who it is who says to you, Give Me a drink, you would have asked Him, and He would have given you living water."* – John 4:10. The Apostle Paul, at Athens, when he found an idol they worshipped with the inscription 'To the unknown God,' said – *"Men of Athens, I perceive that you are very religious."* …. *"Therefore, the one whom you worship without knowing, Him I proclaim to you."* – Acts 17:22-23. He then preached Christ.

(c) Understanding culture

The word 'culture' is a broad term that covers a wide range of topics, including linguistic, social, economic, religious, racial, national, political, psychological, traditional customs, and other differences.

We see several of these applicable when Jesus entered the Nazareth synagogue.

> *"So, He came to Nazareth where He had been brought up. And as His custom was, He went into the synagogue on the Sabbath day and stood up to read."*
>
> Luke 4:16.

We have Jesus' background, race, religion, culture, and customs, to mention a few.

Louis J. Luzbetak, in his book, "The Church and Cultures," says, "that political systems, kinships, family organisation, and law are examples of social adaptation, a plan according to which one is to interact with his fellows. A man copes with his ideational environment through knowledge, art, magic, science, philosophy, and religion. Cultures are different answers to essentially the same human problem."

The object of communicating the gospel of the kingdom in a culture is to communicate Christ so that the people will understand, repent, and believe the gospel.

In our modern world, some churches successfully present the gospel through the arts, drama, movies, and other forms of technology.

The power of persuasion

No matter how skilful we may become in presenting the gospel, the ultimate aim is to persuade people to come to faith and follow Christ. It involves the skill of reasoning to influence people to act.

Paul was out to persuade both Jews and Greeks that Jesus was Lord from the time of his conversion.

"...And confounded the Jews who dwelt in Damascus, proving that this Jesus was the Christ. "And he spoke boldly in the name of the Lord Jesus and disputed (argued) against the Hellenists." (Greek Jews). Acts

9:22 and 29. "And he reasoned in the synagogue every Sabbath and persuaded both Jews and Greeks."

Acts 18:4.

"You almost persuade me to become a Christian."

Acts 26:28.

He almost persuaded him! What a missed opportunity for King Agrippa to become a Christian. It may have been the only opportunity he had; if so, one he would have regretted for all eternity.

A salesman quickly learns how to persuade someone to act and buy their product. What can be greater than the gospel? And it is free. It is worth the effort to try and persuade people to turn to Christ and to follow Him.

The following advantages will aid psychological and communication skills.

Having something Reciprocal -

If we offer someone a gift (such as a pen), they are more likely to feel obligated to give you something back. "A sense of equity and fairness usually drives most people," says Robert Levine.

If we offer the gospel as a gift with benefits, we usually have someone's attention.

Having something in Common -

We have already dealt with this. However, having something in common with the person you are trying to persuade is a distinct advantage.

Having something Scarce -

When people think there is a limited supply of something, they do not want to miss out and are more inclined to want it. Salespeople use this technique to secure a sale. There is no limit to who can enter the kingdom of God, but there can be limited opportunities. Without being deceptive, if people are made aware of this fact, they will be more inclined to commit to following Christ.

I will conclude this section with a quote from David K. Berlo's book, "The Process of Communication: An Introduction to Theory and Practice."

"Our basic purpose in communication is to become an affecting agent, to affect others, our physical environment, and ourselves, and to become a determining agent, to have a vote in how things are. In short, we communicate to influence – to affect with intent."

THE AMBIGUOUS KINGDOM

Chapter 13

Your Kingdom come Your will be done

The heading of this chapter is the central theme of Christian prayer and theology. It expresses the longing for God's kingdom to be fully realised and for His will to be done in our lives both now and in the future.

Responding to the disciple's request, "Lord, teach us to pray." Jesus gave them what is known today as the Lord's Prayer as a guideline for praying. In that prayer, we find the phrase -

> *"Your kingdom come your will be done on earth as it is in heaven...."*
>
> Matthew 6:9.

Jesus clarified that God's will should be done here on earth as it is in Heaven. This is also a call to obedience to His will. Is that even possible? It must be possible; why would Jesus say to pray for it if it were impossible?

When we are willing to obey Him, it is a sign that we have faith in God because we trust Him. As soon as you mention the word obedience, some Christians get their backup and conjure up images of legalism. Can we obey without becoming legalistic?

The battle to obey

We need to be aware that there are two types of obedience: constructive and destructive. Obeying God is always constructive. Obeying God is for our benefit. When we obey Him, He promises to bless us. However, blind obedience can be destructive when a person obeys someone or an organisation out of ignorance or fear, regardless of what they believe to be morally or legally correct. God withdraws His blessing, and they face the consequences of their blind obedience.

It is sometimes difficult to obey God if He asks us to do something that may involve choices we do not like or want to follow.

Jesus Himself, in the garden of Gethsemane, prayed when He knew He would soon face death on the cross. He fell on His face and prayed -

> *"O My Father, if it is possible, let this cup pass from Me; nevertheless, not as I will, but as you will."*
>
> Matthew 26:39.

The cup Jesus is referring to is His impending death on the cross. He is asking the Father if there is another alternative.

If we were facing such a brutal death on the cross at the hands of the Romans, I'm sure we would be seeking another alternative.

Jesus says, *"Not My will, but your will be done."* He knew He must die on the cross as the sacrificial Lamb of God. It is one thing to know the will of God, and it is another to obey. It is interesting to note how Jesus had asked the disciples to watch and pray with Him. When He returned from being a short distance away from them, He found them sleeping and said to Peter – *"What? Could you not watch with Me one hour? Watch and pray, lest you enter into temptation. The spirit indeed is willing, but the flesh is weak."* – Matthew 26:40-41.

Our spirit may be willing to obey, but our flesh is weak and vulnerable to temptation. Obedience is not as easy as it may seem.

In the Old Testament, we read how God rejected King Saul as a leader because he was unwilling to obey Him. God sent Samuel, the prophet who said –

> *"Has the Lord as great delight in burnt offerings and sacrifices, As in obeying the voice of the Lord? Behold to obey is better than sacrifice, and to heed than the fat of rams. For rebellion is as the sin of witchcraft, and stubbornness is as iniquity and idolatry. Because you have rejected the Lord, He has also rejected you from being king."*
>
> 1 Samuel 15:22-23.

Yes, obeying the voice of the Lord is better than sacrifice. Saul spared the king of the Amalekites and also the animals to give them to the people and made a sacrifice to the Lord when God had told him to destroy everything. He thought he was doing the right thing by saving the animals for a sacrifice. But God was not impressed because he had disobeyed his explicit instructions. We may think that is a tough call, but it shows us how God feels about obedience. He wants us to trust Him. We can try to make sacrifices and manipulate things in our favour, thinking we are doing the right thing. It may seem religious and justifiable, but we are in trouble if it is disobedience to God. In the New Testament, we can thank God for His abundant grace that enables us to survive.

We read how the apostle Paul struggled to obey. He indicated that his battle to obey was tough for him because of his fleshly desires and the sin factor at work in his being. A struggle we are all familiar with.

> *"But now it is no longer I who do it, but sin that dwells in me. For I know that in me (that is in my flesh) nothing good dwells; for to will is present with me, but how to perform what is good I do not find. For the good that I will to do, I do not do; but the evil I will not do, that I practice."*
>
> Romans 7:17-19.

Keys to obeying God

C. S. Lewis said, "Obedience is the key that opens every door." But how do we obey without falling into the trap of legalism?

What are some keys to obeying God? I believe there are

several keys.

1. By hearing His voice

Jesus said My sheep, hear My voice. (John 10). As Christians, we listen to the voice of God through His word and the inner witness of the Holy Spirit. We will want to obey when we hear His voice and recognise that the Lord is speaking to us. When the devil tempted Jesus to disobey God, Jesus would quote relevant scriptures saying, *"No"* to the devil by declaring, *"It is written."* – (Matthew 4)

So, to obey Him, we need to hear His voice and be willing to obey it.

2. By loving Him

Jesus said, if you love Me, you will keep my commandments (John 14). We obey God because we love Him. Jesus obeyed His Father because He loved Him. *"But the world may know that I love the Father, and as the Father gave Me commandment, so I do."* – John 14:31.

After Jesus had risen and appeared to the disciples and had breakfast with them. Jesus asked Peter three times, *"Do you love Me?"* Peter was upset because He asked him a third time, "Do you Love Me." Each time, Peter said yes, but to each response, Jesus said, Feed My lambs, Tend My sheep, Feed My sheep. Jesus knew if Peter loved Him, he would obey Him and fulfil his calling as an apostle and shepherd. We obey because we love Him.

3. By walking in the Spirit

Jesus spoke of sending another Helper to us, the Holy Spirit, who would lead and guide us into all truth. (John 14). The apostle Paul tells us nothing can condemn you if you walk in the Spirit. "There is therefore no condemnation to those who are in Christ Jesus, who do not walk according to the flesh, but according to the Spirit." Romans 8:1. In verse 14, it says, "For as many as are led by the Spirit of God, they are the sons of God. Again, Paul says in Galatians 5:16, "Walk in the Spirit, and you will not fulfil the lusts of the flesh."

Paul lists the fruit of the Spirit as love, joy, peace, patience, kindness, goodness, faithfulness, gentleness, and self-control; against these things, there is no law.

Obeying His will is our priority

Sometimes, there is confusion because our church denomination is relative and has variable priorities and rules compared to the kingdom of God, which is absolute.

Jesus said, *"Repent for the kingdom of God is at hand."* – Matthew 4:17.

People do not repent to join a denomination. He did not say repent because your church or particular denomination is at hand. (of course, there were no denominations at the time, but I think you get the point I am trying to make.)

What is your priority? I suggest you should be kingdom-minded before you are denomination-minded. Understand me; I love the church and my denomination. But we betray the kingdom of God if the values of our church override those of the kingdom. They should be the same anyway.

For example, in the early church, some Christians displayed a pharisaical attitude, demanding that sections of the law be applied and upheld.

"But some of the sect of the Pharisees who believed rose up, saying, "It is necessary to circumcise them, and to command them to keep the law of Moses." – Acts 15:5. Paul clarifies this by saying, *"For in Christ Jesus neither circumcision nor uncircumcision avails anything, but a new creation."* – Galatians 6:15.

Some churches may have legalistic or religious rules that do not follow the word of God. We are a new creation in Christ, but we should not try to impress anyone by keeping the law or making self-righteous rules.

Another issue in many denominations is Health and Healing. Some Christians get confused or are influenced by what their denomination teaches. So, to be on the safe side, they pray. "If it be your will, Lord." If it is not the will of God to heal, why did Jesus spend so much time healing people?

"God anointed Jesus of Nazareth with the Holy Spirit and with power, who went about doing good and healing all who were oppressed by the devil," for God was with Him."

Acts 10:38.

Although I have seen many people healed in response to prayer, including myself, I strongly support the medical profession. I believe God can also use it to help us stay fit and healthy so we can continue serving Him.

Historically, the church has been relative and variable in some things, but the kingdom is absolute. However, much of humanity today seeks other solutions and alternatives rather than a willingness to obey God.

Seeking other alternatives

They turn to several ways, such as seeking guidance but not necessarily obedience. They want to be free spirits and seek wisdom and healing through various New Age methods.

Some use tarot cards, horoscopes, fortune tellers, mediums, gurus, etc. In primitive countries, people often seek guidance and healing through sorcery, witchcraft, and ancestral spirits. God warns us to seek Him, not other alternatives.

"And when they say to you, "Seek those who are mediums and wizards, who whisper and mutter," should not a people seek their God? Should they seek the dead on behalf of the living?"

Isaiah 8:19.

Even as Christians, we do some silly things when seeking guidance from God, like I did when I graduated from Bible College.

I desperately sought the Lord's guidance to plant a church in a country town in Victoria. So, I put a map of Victoria on the table, blindfolded myself, spun the map around, and put my finger on it. I was expecting to land in a country town, but to my dismay, it landed in Melbourne, the one place I did not want to go.

To cut a long story short, guess where I ended up? Yes, in Melbourne. It is a dangerous method, and I would never recommend that you do it.

There are much safer ways to seek guidance. We can apply many lessons, but these are a few that have worked for me.

Safe ways to seek guidance

1. An attitude of Prayer

Approach the Lord in prayer like Jesus with an attitude of surrender, saying, "Not my will, but your will be done."

2. Assurance from the word

Look for confirmation as you read and study the word of God.

3. Listen to the Holy Spirit

Be attentive to the Holy Spirit. Jesus said the Spirit would guide us into truth.

4. Inner Peace

We are told in the word to let the peace of God rule our hearts and minds for guidance.

5. Seek wise counsel

Seek counsel from wise people who have been around for a while and are experienced counsellors.

6. Open and closed doors

Confirmation can come through God opening or closing a door of opportunity.

7. Conformation through others

Others can confirm the way you feel God is leading you.

8. Have faith with patience

We need to add some patience to our faith, wait upon God, and not try to take matters into our own hands.

So, next time you pray, "Your Kingdom come, your will be done here on earth as it is in heaven," may you better appreciate what a blessing it is to obey God's will by living in God's kingdom.

Chapter 14

Missions and the gospel of the kingdom

I have had the privilege of being involved in mission work throughout my ministry. 'Missions and the gospel of the kingdom' is the belief and practice within Christian communities of spreading the message of the kingdom of God to people worldwide through various forms of mission work.

This includes not only individual salvation but also the transformation of societies and cultures to embrace the values of the kingdom of God. They express God's love in tangible ways to address poverty, injustice, oppression, and spiritual brokenness.

One of the highlights of our over forty years in ministry was the six years we spent on the mission field in Papua New Guinea.

We were instrumental in establishing a Bible College with the late John Pasterkamp to train national leaders. We were there when God poured out His Holy Spirit throughout the nation. It was an exciting and profitable time that impacted the country.

As a result, many came to faith in Christ, some were healed and delivered, and the kingdom of God spread rapidly, with many churches planted around the nation. However, we live in a changing world. Missions and missionaries stand on the threshold of a new era today.

In his book, "Colonialism and Christian Missions," Steven Neill says, "One age has died; another is striving to be born. We stand in a time of birth pangs, in which the future is still obscure."

Things have become a little clearer since he wrote those words and during our time on the mission field. The most notable is that colonialism has given way to nationalism.

However, as nations gain their independence, a new set of problems arise. Political and economic climates have become unpredictable and unstable.

Missions and missionaries can no longer rely on protection from their colonial authorities. Passport and visa requirements can suddenly change. Military "Coup De Tat" is a dangerous prospect when determining a nation's leadership.

J. Herbert Kane, in his book, "A Global View on Christian Missions," says, "Every sovereign state has the right to exclude or expel anyone deemed undesirable. Many Communist countries have historically closed their doors to the Christian Missionary. Many Muslims have done the same.

Other countries, acting on national self-interest, have passed laws banning or restricting mission activities. Black and brown SAHIBS have replaced the white SAHIBS."

Adjusting to today

Missionaries go into a community, whether overseas or local, to preach and teach about Jesus Christ and the kingdom of God.

The missionaries' first responsibility is to God, to reach people and bring them to faith in Christ. Then, it would be to their church or mission or whoever supports them.

To overcome visa problems for overseas missions, the missionary and the mission sometimes must develop a supportive secondary mission to make way for the gospel.

I will make a brief list of possibilities to help support the cause for the existence of missions.

(a) Building Programmes

The local people often need assistance with building programmes. Skilled builders can help the nationals with planning and choosing materials. Support is also required to fund these projects. In PNG, we received funds from Australia, Holland and other countries.

(b) Health Programmes

A clinic or health programme assisted by doctors or nurses can significantly benefit many areas. Governments are usually favourable to any assistance or expertise they can get. I would also suggest that all missionaries take at least a first aid course, preferably to the standard of a first responder.

(c) Educational Programmes

Education is a priority in many third-world countries. A Christian School would be an excellent benefit for generations to come. Of course, getting something on the ground may be expensive. It would also provide work for national teachers.

(d) Special targeted Projects

There are mission projects that target a primary need. There are too many to mention, but for example, "Open Doors" smuggles Bibles into countries that are not open to Christianity. "Destiny Rescue" rescues mainly young girls out of the prostitution trade in many countries.

(e) Financial support

All of the above requires financial support to get things off the ground, establish them, and keep them going. Support is usually raised mainly through mission organisations, churches, businesses, and individuals.

(f) *Domestic Programmes*

Domestic missions usually involve domestic shelters, food for the hungry, soup kitchens, help for people without homes, assisting refugees, and helping with health issues.

• ***A footnote*** - *Most of the above will involve long-term and short-term missionaries and personnel, which all help to accomplish specific goals. One of the greatest needs is suitable accommodation.*

The Biblical mandate

The biblical mandate to go into the world and preach the gospel of the kingdom has not changed.

Proclamation is paramount -

"This gospel of the kingdom will be preached all over the world as a witness to all nations, and then the end will come."

Matthew 24:14.

The practical purpose of the proclamation of the gospel of the kingdom is to bring people out of darkness and a lost eternity into the light of the eternal kingdom of God.

When Jesus came preaching the gospel, it is said,

"The people who sat in darkness have seen a great light. And upon those who sat in the region and shadow of death, Light has dawned."

Matthew 4:16.

Jesus sent the apostle Paul to the Gentiles with the same

mission to bring people out of darkness into the Light.

> *"...I now send you to open their eyes in order to turn them from darkness to light, and from the power of Satan to God, that they may receive forgiveness of sins, and an inheritance among those who are sanctified by faith in Me.*

Acts 26:19-18.

In some cases, when the door closes to missionaries and missions, the nationals are left with buildings and facilities that need extensive maintenance and finance to keep functioning. The mission may now depend upon raising support for the nationals to continue proclaiming the gospel.

Conflict is inevitable -

Preaching the gospel in an unpredictable, changing world is a challenge, especially in developing countries, and can sometimes result in hostility, which may result in inevitable conflict.

It is part of the package for some missionaries and missions. Jesus implied persecution could be something many Christians may experience.

> *"Beware of men, for they will deliver you up to councils and scourge you in their synagogues. You will be brought before governors and kings for My sake as a testimony to them and to the Gentiles."*

Matthew 10:17-18.

Strangely enough, church denominations were responsible

for many of the conflicts we faced on the mission field in PNG. They were very protective of their particular area. In some remote areas, they would take up arms to threaten us if we encroached on their territory.

Some of these conflicts even erupted into some traditional tribal fighting, resulting in some deaths. It probably relates to the conventional tribal fighting that has gone on in some areas for centuries.

The need to be Faithful and adaptable -

Missionaries and missions must learn to be faithful and adapt to conditions they may not like.

I remember preaching in a remote area of the Highlands of PNG, where the temperatures varied greatly. It was hot during the day but very cold at night.

We were preaching at night, and most of the people were wearing what the local missionary called 'green candles,' he was describing the snot hanging from their noses.

Yes, you guessed it. Some would wipe their nose with their hands and then stick them out for you to hug them or shake them.

Rather than offend them, you just had to adapt, grin, and bear it, then ensure you had a good wash when you returned to the missionary's house.

Sometimes, missionaries work in political and social conditions that are not conducive to their normal lifestyle, so they must adapt to those conditions to be faithful.

Missionaries must try to make the gospel as straightforward as possible. Sometimes, acting out stories or illustrations will help people understand the gospel.

The people in PNG loved it when you demonstrated the point you were trying to make by acting it out. Most of the time, the response was overwhelming. Occasionally, people would start coming forward for prayer before you finished preaching.

If possible, the missionary should avoid unfamiliar clichés. I remember saying, "I threw the baby out with the bathwater," the people took it literally and were horrified. You can quickly lose their attention if you are not careful.

Paul said, *"I planted, Apollos watered, but God gave the increase. So then neither he who plants is anything, nor he who waters, but God who gives the increase."* – 1 Corinthians 3:6-7.

The above scripture provides a process that can apply to our conversion experience. There seems to be both a 'point' and a 'process' decision.

The 'point' decision is usually a radical instant change at the point of making a decision, like Saul, who became the Apostle Paul.

"As he journeyed, he came near Damascus, and suddenly a light shone around him from heaven. Then he fell to the ground and heard a voice saying to him, "Saul, Saul, why are you persecuting Me?" And he said,

Missions and the gospel of the kingdom

> *"Who are You, Lord?" Then the Lord said, "I am Jesus who you are persecuting..."*
>
> Acts 9:3-5.

Of course, an experience like this would be rare today, but it gives us a picture of a sudden dramatic change at the conversion point.

The other is the 'process' decision. It occurs when a person converts to Christianity over some time. Most people know when this is happening, but some do not. They only know that something changed within their hearts and minds. But the Lord knows when and how this happens, even if the person is vague.

Allen R. Tippett, in his book, "Theology in Missionary Theology," lists five stages to a conversion 'process.'

1. **Discovery** (discovering Christ).

2. **Deliberation** (forsaking old ways to follow)

3. **Determination** (repentance and faith)

4. **Dissonance** (hesitation – will I continue)

5. **Discipline** (submission to His Lordship)

Whatever the case, whether a 'point' decision or a 'process' decision, the missionaries and missions are responsible for proclaiming the gospel of the kingdom, for it is God who gives the increase.

Missionaries need to set an example for other leaders and believers. I know one missionary who used to Lord it over the nationals with a superior attitude. It was like he had his little kingdom. He once told me, "The only way they will get rid of me is in a box." Fortunately, that did not happen, but some years later, he realised he needed to hand it over to the nationals, and he reluctantly left. But he did well as a pioneer in establishing a great mission and led well spiritually. He has left a great legacy for the nationals to continue to spread the gospel of the kingdom.

Paul says to Timothy, *"Let no one despise your youth; be an example to the believers in word, in conduct, in love, in spirit, in faith, in purity. Till I come, give attention to reading, exhortation, to doctrine."* – 1 Timothy 4:12-13.

In other words, grow up spiritually and be a good example for others to follow.

Oswald J. Sanders, in his book "Spiritual Leadership," says, "Appointment of men with a secular or materialistic outlook prevents the Holy Spirit from carrying out His programme for the church in the world. The Holy Spirit does not take control of any man or body of men against their will. When He sees men elected to positions of leadership who lack spiritual fitness to co-operate with Him, He quietly withdraws and leaves them to implement their own policy according to their own standards, but without His aid."

Chapter 15

When can we expect the coming kingdom?

The timing of Jesus's second coming has been controversial among Christians since the early church. It has been the topic of Christian debate throughout the centuries.

I remember a well-known minister who thought he had it all worked out from his interpretation of scripture and had charts to prove it. There was only one problem: he would have to change his charts when things did not go according to his predictions.

I remember him indicating that when all the planets lined up in 1982 (called the Grand Alignment by Scientists), it would be the time for Christ to return. When that did not happen, he started to focus on the year 2000, which was at the end of a millennium. I think he gave up after that failed to occur.

The Pharisees asked Jesus when the kingdom of God would come. It would have been at the top of their list of questions. Jesus answered -

"The kingdom of God does not come with observation; nor will they say, "See here!" or "See there!" For indeed, the kingdom of God is within you." (or among you).

Luke 17:20-21.

You may as well throw away all your charts and calculations; it cannot be worked out by observation.

I like what Bob Mumford used to say, "I believe in the PAN theory." "It will all PAN out in the end."

This does not mean we should ignore signs leading up to Christ's coming. It is a fascinating subject and worthy of exploration.

Signs of His coming

The Bible does not say when He will come, but we should watch for signs. Jesus tells the parable of the fig tree as an analogy.

"Now learn this parable from the fig tree: When its branch has already become tender and puts forth leaves, you know that summer is near. So, when you see all these things, you know that it is near the doors!"

Matthew 24:32-33.

You know summer is near when the fig tree puts forth its

new leaves. So, Jesus is saying when you see sure signs, you know His return is near.

In the gospels, Jesus gives us a comprehensive list of signs. I will not try to interpret them in any order. They include unpredictable world events, nation against nation, kingdom against kingdom, famines, pestilences, earthquakes, wars and rumours of war, deception, tribulation, persecution of Christians, lawlessness, false prophets, and false Christs. Immediately after giving us the signs and the fig tree parable, Jesus clarifies that nobody knows the actual day or the hour of His coming.

> *"But of that day and hour, no one knows, not even the angels of heaven, but My Father only."*
>
> Matthew 24:36.

Jesus warns us to be watching and to be ready. The implication is that some will become slack, backslide, and return to worldly ways. Jesus likens this to an unfaithful servant, saying –

> *"But if that evil servant says in his heart, "My master is delaying his coming," and begins to beat his fellow servants and to eat and drink with the drunkards, the master of that servant will come on a day when he is not looking for him and at an hour that he is not aware of."*
>
> Matthew 24:48-50.

Notice how it says, *"My master is delaying his coming."* So, we can only discern the signs with some speculation. Many

Christians wonder why there is a delay because many of these signs have been around for a long time.

Why is it taking so long?

When we anticipate that something is going to happen a long way off in the future we glibly say "till kingdom come." This is a cynical way of expressing that it will take forever. Many Christians feel that way about the coming kingdom.

When we are continually waiting for what appears to be a delay in His coming it causes a lot of speculation among Christians.

The apostle Peter predicted this would become an issue in the last days.

> *"Scoffers will come in the last days, walking according to their own lusts, and saying, Where, is the promise of His coming? For since the fathers fell asleep, all things continue as they were from the beginning of creation."*
>
> 2 Peter 3:3-4.

The question is, why is the promise of His coming taking so long? We are some 2000 years down the track. Although there are some signs, there seems to be no hard evidence to support His coming at this stage. Peter goes on to answer this question.

> *"The Lord is not slack concerning His promise, as some count slackness, but is longsuffering toward us, not willing that any should perish but that all should come to repentance. But the day of the Lord*

will come as a thief in the night."

2 Peter 3:9-10.

We learn a few things from the above scriptures to help us process the delay factor.

Firstly, some will use this issue to mock the authority of the word of God in the last days. It will give them an excuse to eat, drink, be merry, and live an ungodly lifestyle as though He will never return.

Secondly, The Lord is not slack but patient and merciful, delaying His coming so that more people will hopefully repent and come to faith in Christ.

Thirdly, We are told to watch and be ready. The Day of the Lord will come.

So far, so good

We need to pause to recap and understand that we are on track, and so far, so good.

The Old Testament prophets had spoken of a coming king (Messiah) and His kingdom, which was to come. Isaiah prophesied of both his first and second coming.

> *"Therefore, the Lord Himself will give you a sign: Behold the virgin shall conceive and bear a Son, and shall call His name Immanuel."*

Isaiah 7:14.

In the New Testament, Matthew quotes this scripture from

Isaiah and applies it to the Virgin Mary and the birth of Jesus.

"And she shall bring forth a Son, and you shall call His name Jesus, for He will save His people from their sins." So, all this was done so that it might be fulfilled, which was spoken by the prophet: "Behold the virgin shall be with child, and bear a Son, and they shall call His name Immanuel, which is translated as "God with us."

Matthew 1:21-23.

This refers to Jesus's first coming. Then, we have another scripture in Isaiah 9: 6-7 that mentions both comings.

"For unto us a child is born, unto us a Son is given; and the government will be upon His shoulder. And His name will be called Wonderful, Counsellor, Mighty God, Everlasting Father, Prince of Peace. Of the increase of His Government and peace, there will be no end. Upon the throne of David and over His kingdom, to order it and establish it with judgment and justice from that time forward, even forever."

We have the birth of Christ at His first coming, then what will happen at His second coming, where the increase of His government will occur, and He will be on the throne of David and rule over His kingdom forever.

The kingdom is at hand

The kingdom of God has various stages. Now, we will outline what I have termed the four phases of the kingdom.

1. The Announcement

John the Baptist announces the kingdom of God. "Repent

for the kingdom of heaven is at hand!" For this is he who was spoken by the prophet Isaiah, saying: "The voice of one crying in the wilderness: Prepare the way of the Lord; Make His paths straight." Matthew 2-3. John is baptising people to prepare for the coming Messiah.

2. *The Inauguration*

Jesus enters the scene to confirm that He is the Messiah, following John the Baptist. *"After John was put in prison, Jesus came to Galilee, preaching the gospel of the kingdom of God, and saying, "The time is fulfilled, and the kingdom of God is at hand. Repent, and believe in the gospel."* – Mark 1:14-15.

Through His earthly ministry, Jesus repeatedly confirmed that He was the Son of God, the expected Messiah.

But to save us, He had to die on the cross and shed His blood as the sacrificial Lamb of God.

It was something the people were not expecting.

But in doing so, He has secured eternal salvation for all who will come to Him and confess that He is their Saviour and Lord.

3. *The Continuation*

We live in the church age. It is an age of grace. The kingdom of God continues to be proclaimed by the church during this time. *"This gospel of the kingdom will be preached in all the world as a witness to all the nations, and then the end will come."* – Matthew 24:14.

4. The Consummation

At the second coming of Christ, when He returns to this earth, He will consummate the kingdom of God.

When Jesus ascended to heaven, two angels appeared and said, *"Men of Galilee, why do you stand gazing up into heaven? This same Jesus who was taken up from you into heaven will so come in like manner as you saw Him go into heaven."* – Acts 1:9-11.

What about Israel?

Someone recently asked me, "Does God still have a plan for Israel?" "If so, does it have any bearing on end-time events leading up to Christ's return?"

As long as Israel has existed, it has consistently endured persecution by its neighbours. God has a plan for Israel and has favoured it as a nation. Satan has always tried to incite hatred toward the Jews and Israel because he wants to destroy them as a nation.

There is much turmoil still in Israel today. It is under constant attack by Hamas, Islamic Jihad, and Hezbollah, who are often sheltered by Palestinian territories (Gaza Strip and the West Bank), Syria, Iran, Lebanon, and others.

It seems that this conflict will continue and become a significant issue that may affect the world until the return of Christ. I will not try to sort out possible scenarios, as others have been doing, except to say God made a covenant with Abraham concerning the Jews having land and living in it as the nation of Israel. The enemies of Israel dispute the land Israel claims to be theirs.

Three theories held by many Christians -

1. Israel and the Church

God has a plan for earthly Israel and spiritual Israel, the church. The focus is on both natural Israel and spiritual Israel (the church), and that plan will continue until the return of Christ.

2. The church supersedes Israel

God dealt with Israel until the cross of Christ, but now His priority is the church in this dispensation of grace until Christ returns.

3. Israel turning to Christ

Despite the majority of Jews having rejected Christ, they must now turn to Christ as their Messiah to become a part of the Bride of Christ, the church.

Hope for a revival in Israel –

"And I will pour out on the house of David and the inhabitants of Jerusalem a Spirit of grace and supplication. They will look on Me, whom they pierced. Yes, they will mourn for Him as one mourns for his only son, and grieve for Him as one grieves for a firstborn."

Zechariah 12:10.

This undoubtedly refers to the Jews recognising that Christ was indeed the Messiah.

The wrong question

Have we been too preoccupied with trying to answer the wrong question? Instead of speculating about the actual time of His return, shouldn't we focus more on what His return will look like and whether we are ready?

Sure, it is our responsibility to observe the signs of His coming, which indicate the closeness of His coming, but not to become too preoccupied and dogmatic about these things.

After all, Jesus said, *"But of that day and hour no one knows, not even the angels of heaven, but My Father only" "Watch, therefore, for you do not know what hour your Lord is coming." "Therefore, you also be ready, for the Son of Man is coming at an hour you do not expect." –* Matthew 24:36-44.

In the next chapter, we will focus more on what to expect when He comes. What will it look like?

Chapter 16

How will the King and His kingdom return?

Christians all over the world are eagerly awaiting the return of Christ. It is universally accepted.

The Nicene Creed is a detailed statement of faith that most Christian denominations adhere to. A section in it states that Jesus and His kingdom will return. Let me quote that part.

"On the third day, He rose again in accordance with the scriptures; He ascended into heaven and is seated at the right hand of the Father. He will come again in glory to judge the living and the dead, and His kingdom will have no end."

It is something that all Christians anticipate. But how will this unfold? What can we expect?

The free encyclopedia Wikipedia states —

"The second coming (sometimes called the second advent

or the Parousia) is the Christian belief that Jesus Christ will return to Earth after His ascension to Heaven (which is said to have occurred about two thousand years ago). The idea is based on Messianic prophesies and is part of most Christian eschatology. Other faiths have various interpretations of it."

Despite many interpretations and theories about the return of Christ and His kingdom, there remains an element of mystery and speculation concerning these events. Christians are encouraged to stay vigilant, faithful, and hopeful while awaiting His return. What can we expect?

All will see His return

How did Jesus describe His second coming? There are many references, but let's take one and make some comments.

> *"Therefore, if they say to you, "Look, He is in the desert!" do not go out; or "Look, He is in the inner rooms!" Do not believe it. As the lightning comes from the east and flashes to the west, so will the coming of the Son of Man be."*
>
> Matthew 24:26-27.

It is a spectacular event that everyone will see. Just as lightning lights up the sky, it will be like this when Jesus returns.

The word 'coming' can be translated from the Greek as Parousia, which means presence or arrival. In ancient times, it described the visit of a ruler to a city, with all the festive atmosphere surrounding such a visit.

Is there a secret rapture?

The rapture is an eschatological position held by some Christians where all the dead believers will be resurrected and joined by believers still alive on earth. Together, they will rise and be "caught up" in the clouds to meet the Lord in the air. They go to a prepared place where they escape the great tribulation for seven years before returning with the Lord.

Some will interpret the scriptures to indicate a secret rapture that involves the *"catching up"* of believers before the great tribulation. The word rapture is from the Latin word raptus, meaning *"caught up,"* or in Greek, it means *"to snatch away,"* as in 1 Thessalonians 4:17.

This secret rapture theory became popular because of how the Scofield Reference Bible interpreted the scriptures about the second coming.

Two books added to the popularity, one by Hal Lindsey, "The Late Great Planet Earth," and another by Jerry Jenkins and Tim LaHaye, "Left Behind." "Left Behind: The Movie," based on the book, made the rapture theory widely known.

In the movie, planes were falling out of the sky, cars, trucks, buses, and trains were crashing, and people on earth were killed as Christian pilots and drivers disappeared in the rapture.

All of this hype resulted in a variety of bumper stickers seen around the world, such as, "When I am taken up in the rapture, you can have my car," "Warning: if this car has no driver, the rapture has taken place," "In case of the rapture this car will be unmanned."

It would undoubtedly cause a lot of havoc with believers suddenly disappearing. You can imagine the chaos. There would be accident upon accident, causing death and destruction all over the world.

One thing is for sure: there would be nothing secret about it. If there is a rapture, you cannot miss it; everybody will be aware of it.

For and against the rapture

One of the critical scriptures used to support the rapture is one Paul writes to mainly comfort those grieving the loss of loved ones.

> *"For if we believe that Jesus died and rose again, even so, God will bring with Him those who sleep in Jesus. For this, we say to you, by the word of the Lord, that we who are alive and remain until the coming of the Lord will by no means precede those who are asleep. For the Lord Himself will descend from heaven with a shout, with the voice of an archangel, and with the trumpet of God. And the dead in Christ will rise first. Then we who remain alive will be caught up with them in the clouds to meet the Lord in the air. And thus, we shall always be with the Lord. Therefore, comfort one another with these words."*
>
> 1 Thessalonians 4:14-18.

The theory is that when this church age (or the age of grace) finishes, the dead believers and those still alive are "caught up" to meet the Lord in the air. They do not descend to earth but go to a place prepared for them, where they escape the great tribulation. After seven years of tribulation, they return with the Lord (the second coming), and the millennium begins.

Another scripture used to support this theory, which is often quoted and linked to this one, is Matthew 24: 29-31 – *"Immediately after the tribulation of those days....and they will see the Son of Man coming on the clouds of heaven with power and great glory. And He will send His angels with a great sound of a trumpet, and they will gather together His elect from the four winds, from one end of heaven to the other."*

Even though the rapture theory seems plausible and likable, I am not entirely convinced of the interpretation of the scriptures used to support it.

Most Christian denominations do not subscribe to the rapture theory. They differ in their interpretation of the aerial gathering described in 1 Thessalonians 4:17. They do not use 'rapture' as a theological term. Instead, they interpret it as the elect gathering with Christ at the time of His second coming.

Whatever we believe about the existence and timing of the Second Coming does not justify hostility toward those with different opinions. Jesus commanded us to love one another if we are to have an impact on the world.

Coming in the clouds

There seems to be one common denominator regarding Christ's return. He is coming in the clouds. This has no hidden or secret meaning; He will come from heaven to earth with the clouds, and every eye will see Him.

> *"Behold He is coming with clouds, and every eye will see Him, even they who pierced Him. And all the tribes of the earth will mourn because of Him. Even so, Amen."*
>
> Revelation 1:7

Daniel recorded that He was coming with the clouds of heaven to establish His kingdom.

> *"One like the Son of man, coming with the clouds of heaven! He came to the Ancient of Days, and they brought Him near before Him. Then to Him was given dominion and glory and a kingdom, that all peoples, nations, and languages should serve Him. His dominion is an everlasting dominion, which shall not pass away, and His kingdom the one that shall not be destroyed."*
>
> Daniel 7:13-14.

When Jesus ascended back to heaven in the clouds, the angels said to those gazing up -

> *"This same Jesus, who was taken up from you into heaven, will come in like manner as you saw Him go into heaven."*
>
> Acts 1:11.

Paul expounds the second coming

In 1 and 2 Thessalonians, Paul's theme throughout these two books focuses on the Second Coming and related behaviour for believers as we wait.

I will outline and highlight some of these thoughts from

each chapter.

1 Thess 1 – As believers, we will escape the wrath to come.

"And you became followers of us and of the Lord, having received the word in much affliction, with the joy of the Holy Spirit. You turned to God from idols to serve the living and true God, and to wait for His Son from heaven, whom He raised from the dead, even Jesus who delivers us from the wrath to come."

1 Thess 2 – Our converts will be our crown of rejoicing at His coming.

"We have suffered tribulation"

"But what is our hope, or joy, or crown of rejoicing? Is it not even you in the presence of our Lord Jesus Christ at His Coming?" For you are our glory and Joy."

1 Thess 3 – May we be blameless in holiness at His coming.

"Despite many afflictions that you may increase and abound in love"

"That He may establish your hearts blameless in holiness before our God and Father at the coming of the Lord Jesus Christ with all His saints."

1 Thess 4 – May we comfort those who grieve the loss of loved ones.

"And the dead in Christ will rise first. Then we who are alive and remain shall be caught up together with them in the clouds to meet

the Lord in the air. And thus, we shall always be with the Lord." "Therefore, comfort one another with these words."

1 Thess 5 – May our spirit, soul, and body be blameless at His coming.

"Now may the God of peace sanctify you completely, and may your whole spirit, soul, and body be preserved blameless at the coming of our Lord Jesus Christ."

2 Thess 1 – He is coming with His mighty angels in flaming fire to take vengeance.

"It is a righteous thing for God to repay with tribulation those who trouble you"

"When the Lord Jesus is revealed from heaven with His mighty angels in flaming fire taking vengeance on those who do not know God, and on those who do not obey the gospel" "When He comes in that day to be glorified in His saints and be admired by all those who believe."

2 Thess 2 -The man of sin revealed, but destroyed at His coming

"Now concerning the coming of the Lord Jesus Christ do not be troubled" "the man of sin will be revealed who opposes and exalts himself above all that is called God" "Whom the Lord will consume with the breath of His mouth and destroy with the brightness of His coming."

2 Thess 3 – Despite the idleness of some, do not grow weary in doing good.

"If anyone will not work, neither shall he eat. "For we hear that there are some who walk among you in a disorderly manner, not working at all, but are busybodies."

"But as for you, brethren, do not grow weary in doing good.".

Not left without an ending

How will it all end? Some movies have no definitive ending. You are left hanging and have to work it out for yourself. However, Christians are not in limbo without an ending. As Christians, we have a great ending to look forward to: the return of Christ.

F.E. Brunner, in The Christian doctrine of the church, Faith and the Consummation: Dogmatics, Vol 3. "This thought of the future is anything but superfluous mythology…" "Faith in Jesus without the expectation of His Parousia is a cheque that is never cashed, a promise that is not made in earnest. A faith in Christ without the expectation of a Parousia is like a flight of stairs that leads nowhere but ends in the void."

In other words, what's the point of it all if we are without a climax or a satisfactory ending? But we are not to worry; God has it all planned out, and it will be the grand finale of our Christian experience.

If I were to sum up how He will return in a nutshell, I would declare Christ will come visibly in the clouds, and every eye will see Him. He will eventually separate the sheep from the goats, deal with His enemies, set up His kingdom, judge the living and the dead, and reward the faithful, issue in the

New Jerusalem, New Heaven, and New Earth.

The final consummation

The final consummation is in the book of Revelation. It is a fascinating book that has caused much speculation about the correct interpretation of the book and how it applies to followers of Christ.

I do not want to enter that arena except to say that Christ is the primary focus. Many want to put the whole book somewhere in the future. For example, the messages directed to the seven churches in Asia were too literal churches in that period. But it does not mean we cannot learn lessons from these messages that may also apply to us.

If we were to study history, we would probably find that much of Revelation may already have its place in history. However, we can learn spiritual lessons once we look into these events.

If you want an interesting in-depth study of revelation, I recommend Dr. Andrew Corbett's book, "The Most Embarrassing Book in the Bible." However, without trying to interpret the sequence of events, we are dealing with references in Revelation about the coming of Christ.

Who is, who was, who is to come -

What an opening statement in the first chapter!

"I am the Alpha and Omega, the Beginning and the End." Says the Lord, "Who is and who was and who is to come, the Almighty."

Revelation 1:8.

The Lord, who is (ever-present), who was (on earth and is now in heaven), and who is to come (yet to return to this earth), as the Almighty to reign and rule forever.

We are familiar with the one who was and the one who is. So, let us focus on the one who is to come, which concerns events surrounding Christ's return and His kingdom.

King of Kings and Lord of Lords -

We have a description of Christ coming on a white horse with the armies of heaven to judge and make war against those who oppose Him.

"Now out of His mouth goes a sharp sword, that with it He should smite the nations. And he Himself will rule them with a rod of iron. He Himself treads the winepress of the fierceness and wrath of Almighty God. And He has on His robe and on His thigh a name written: KING OF KINGS AND LORD OF LORDS."

Revelation 19:15-16.

He will judge and make war against the beast, the false prophet, the kings of the earth, the nations, the Devil (Satan), and his hordes.

It appears to be in conjunction with His coming. Some would say the battle of Armageddon.

It is a far cry from His first coming as the sacrificial Lamb of God, who shed His blood on the cross so we could all find forgiveness of sins and eternal life in preparation for the future.

The one-thousand-year reign –

The sequence of events unfolding in the Book of Revelation is controversial. Some say we are already in the millennium. However, we have the one-thousand-year reign with Christ referred to as the millennium; Satan is to be bound and cast into the bottomless pit but released for a short time after that period has expired.

The Great white throne –

Then comes the great white throne judgment, where all the dead are judged according to their works written in the "Books." But whoever is not found in the "Book of Life" will be cast into the lake of fire.

New Jerusalem, New Heaven, and New Earth -

We now come to the final consummation of the Kingdom, the New Jerusalem, the New Heaven, and the New Earth, something we are all looking forward to, which must be the ultimate event for all Christians.

"Now I saw a new heaven and a new earth, for the first heaven and the first earth had passed away. Also, there was no more sea."

"Then I, John, saw the holy city, New Jerusalem, coming down out of heaven from God, prepared as a bride adorned for her husband. And I heard a loud voice from heaven saying, "Behold the tabernacle of God is with men, and he will dwell with them, and they shall be His people.""

How will the King and His kingdom return?

God Himself will be with them and be their God. And God will wipe away every tear from their eyes; there shall be no more death, nor sorrow, nor crying. There shall be no more pain for the former things have passed away."

Revelation 21:1-4.

How good is that? No more tears, death, sorrow, crying, or pain. What an honour to Live with God in the Glorious atmosphere of the new Jerusalem.

I believe it is a natural, tangible place, both literal and spiritual. We will not be like disembodied spirits. We will all have immortal bodies.

In the last chapter, we have this reassurance. *"And there shall be no more curse, but the throne of God and of the Lamb shall be in it, and His servants shall serve Him. They shall see His face, and His name shall be on their foreheads. There shall be no night there: They need no lamp nor light of the sun, for the Lord God gives them light. And they shall reign forever and ever."* – Revelation 22:3-5.

I do not think we can fully comprehend what this will be like. What an environment. But whatever you can imagine, it is bound to be better. It will also be when all the saints will be rewarded for their service here on earth.

"And behold I am coming quickly, and My reward is with Me, to give to everyone according to his work."

Revelation 22:12.

An invitation to come -

We have this wonderful invitation to all who hear and are thirsty. Come and drink!

> *"I, Jesus, have sent My angel to testify to you these things in the churches. I am the Root and the Offspring of David, the Bright and Morning Star." "And the Spirit and the bride say, "Come!" And let him who hears say, "Come!" And let him who thirsts come. Whoever desires, let him take the water of life freely."*
>
> Revelation 22:16-17.

By the grace of God, this is an invitation for anyone to come. It is a gift and an opportunity for you to come to faith in Christ.

Chapter 17

As you see the day approaching

What should we be doing as we see the day of the Lord approaching? How should we prepare for that day?

We must understand that the day of the Lord will be a terrible day of judgment and sudden destruction for the unprepared.

> *"For you yourselves know perfectly that the day of the Lord so comes as a thief in the night. When they say, "Peace and safety!" then sudden destruction comes upon them, as labour pains upon a pregnant woman. And they shall not escape." "But you brethren are not in darkness, so that this day should overtake you as a thief."*
>
> 1 Thessalonians 5:2-4.

Yes, there will come a day of sudden destruction for the ungodly. The Book of Jude reminds us of this coming great day of judgment. (It is worth reading the whole book to absorb the context.)

Although Christians are aware of this, some still become complacent because they live in a state of peace and safety. Christians need to be careful not to become careless and slide back to their old ways.

Urged to stay in fellowship

Christians are urged to stay in fellowship by attending a local church.

> *"Let us hold fast the confession of our hope without wavering, for He who promised is faithful. And let us consider one another in order to stir up love and good works, not forsaking the assembling of ourselves together, as is the manner of some, but exhorting one another, and so much more as you see the day approaching."*
>
> Hebrews 10:23-25.

I remember preaching this passage some time ago, and someone challenged me and said, "All you want to see is an increase in numbers in your church because you are afraid of losing people." I had to agree that they were partially correct, but I assured them it was not my motive. I did not want to see people lose interest in church, drift away, and backslide because of a lack of fellowship.

It is a touchy subject because some people have been hurt, wounded, or abused because of their involvement in a church, and they find it hard to stay in fellowship. They still love the Lord but are missing out on much-needed fellowship.

We need to remember that we are living in days of

deception where the devil desires to destroy our fellowship with one another. Jesus implies that the devil knows a divided kingdom (or church) cannot stand. (Matthew 12:25-26).

The church is a miniature plant of the kingdom of God on earth; we need to be united and part of it if we hope to impact the world.

It is so easy to drift away

I have noticed over the years that many Christians fall into the trap of drifting away without initially making a deliberate decision to turn away from God or the church. It is often through neglect. If we neglect to water our garden, things will eventually die. If we neglect our relationship with God and others, we are in danger of dying spiritually.

> *"Therefore, we must give the more earnest heed to the things we have heard, lest we drift away." "How shall we escape if we neglect so great a salvation, which at the first began to be spoken by the Lord and was confirmed to us by those who heard Him."*
>
> Hebrews 2:1-3.

Drifting away is slipping away without deliberately deciding to do so. It usually happens because someone has been lured or distracted by something that has drawn believers away from regular fellowship.

When I was pastoring, a family in the church bought a speed boat and started skiing. It was fine initially, and often, it was entertainment on a Saturday for church people. However, as time passed, they started skiing on Sundays and gradually drifted away from attending church.

I am not suggesting they lost their salvation, but they may be putting themselves in danger of doing so. What is certain is that they will miss out on fellowship with other dedicated Christians and the benefits of that experience.

Benefits of assembling together

In our scripture in Hebrews 10:19-25, many benefits are gained from fellowshipping with other Christians.

I will list several benefits I have gleaned from the above passage of scripture.

1. A clear conscience to approach God.
2. Support to stand on the promises of God.
3. Stir one another up for love and good works.
4. Less likely to drift away from God.
5. Find encouragement through one another.

I know the church does not always live up to its potential, but we must be careful not to develop a critical spirit towards the church. The church is God's idea. The head of the church is Jesus, described as the bridegroom who lovingly laid down His life for the church, His cherished bride.

The church should not be considered just another artificial institution (even if it sadly acts that way sometimes). The church comprises people like you and me, sinners saved by grace who have responded to the call of Christ. The church is God ordained for our benefit and survival, especially in the last days as we see the day of the Lord approaching. Another distinct advantage of fellowship is that Christians can discuss and assess world events and the signs of His return. They can also discern doctrine and cater to practical needs relevant to living and surviving in the last days.

Sober warnings

We are soberly warned not to play with sacred things related to the Christian faith and our relationship with God. Our walk with Christ should not be taken lightly.

"Of how much worse punishment, do you suppose, will he be thought worthy who has trampled the Son of God underfoot, counted the blood of the covenant by which he was sanctified a common thing, and insulted the Spirit of grace? For we know Him who said, "Vengeance is Mine, I will repay," And again, "The Lord will judge His people." It is a fearful thing to fall into the hands of the living God."

Hebrews 10:29-30.

If we reject or oppose the gospel, we insult the Spirit of grace God has offered us for our salvation and find ourselves in serious trouble.

"How shall we escape if we neglect so great a salvation."

Hebrews 2:3.

We also risk insulting the Spirit of grace when we neglect

our salvation. In this context, neglect means that one is not as concerned as one should be, and as a result, one has become careless and drifted away from God, neglecting so great a salvation.

Are you ready?

We do not want to be caught off guard!

> *"Therefore, you also be ready, for the Son of Man is coming at an hour you do not expect."*
>
> Matthew 24:44.

If you are reading this and feel unprepared, there is still time to put things right; the door is not closed.

The invitation is for all races, ethnicities, and kinds of people. No one is too different, too sinful, too disabled, or too good to be invited by the grace of God to come. God desires to fill His kingdom with people from all over the world, including you.

You have an opportunity right now to come to faith in Christ. Open your heart, ask Christ to forgive you, and I will give you a prayer to repeat.

Repeat this prayer -

"Lord Jesus, I come to you and ask for your forgiveness; I confess that I am a sinner and need your gift of salvation. Come into my heart and make me a new person. I confess by faith that you are now my Saviour and Lord."

If you have prayed this prayer and meant it with all your heart, I welcome you to the kingdom of God.

Remember, understanding the kingdom of God is an ongoing journey of growth and discovery. Thank you for reading this book. May we continue to spread the gospel of the kingdom of God together.

www.ingramcontent.com/pod-product-compliance
Lightning Source LLC
Chambersburg PA
CBHW031248290426
44109CB00012B/490